Here Am I; Send Me
Answering God's Call to Ministry

KAREN HARRIS, MSN

Published in Chicago, Illinois by Wealth and Riches Today 1074 West Taylor Street, Suite 335, Chicago, IL 60607.

Wealth and Riches Today is a registered trademark of Wealth and Riches Today, Inc. Chicago, IL 60607. Office: 312.493.4770
Email: lrenee.richardson@wealthandrichestoday.com

Wealth and Riches Today titles may be purchased in bulk for educational, business, fund-raising, or sales promotional use, please email lrenee.richardson@wealthandrichestoday.com.

Unless otherwise indicated, all Scripture quotations are taken from the King James Version (KJV) of the Holy Bible.

ISBN-13:978-0692995907
ISBN-10:0692995900

Library of Congress Cataloging in Publication
Library of Congress Control Number: 2017962959
Printed in the United States of America

Interior Design
Signature Designer: Shirri Buchanan.

Photography
Glen Richardson, Monet Studios.

2017 first Edition

CHICAGO \\ ATLANTA \\ NEW YORK \\ CAPE TOWN

To

Moselean Parker

From

Karen Ha___

Special Note

I pray that this book
is a blessing to you!
Thank you for your
support

An Introduction to
Evangelist Karen Harris

I am excited to introduce you to our anointed author Evangelist Karen Harris. She is a powerful woman of God, who has heard the voice of the Lord call her for the work of the ministry.

When Karen realized the voice of the Lord was calling her for service, it was hard for her to understand why he had chosen her. She continued to hear His calling to share the gospel with a dying world. She felt overwhelmed by the call and at first hesitated to go. Fortunately for the many lives she has touched, she began to obey His voice and could not take it lightly. As the urgency of the call increased, finally she said, Here am I; Lord, Send me. She had to answer the call.

I remember the first day I met Evangelist Harris. I saw her singing joyously in the choir. At the end of the service she immediately came to me and introduced herself as the first lady's sister and the pastor's sister-in-law. She said I know God sent you to support our wonderful pastor and his wife. She also said I was sent to be a spiritual support for her too. I knew God had a call on her life. I received our pastor's blessing to become her mentor and I became a spiritual mother to her.

We began to travel and attend different conferences in Chicago and cities across the country. We spent a lot of time together and our spiritual mother-daughter relationship began to grow and grow. We were Ruth and Naomi. We were Elizabeth and Mary. I have watched her grow by leaps and bounds as she continued to obey the voice of the Lord and carry his word to this generation.

Therefore I pray and thank those of you who read this book. I hope you will find it to be insightful, thought provoking and a resource for your growth. Please enjoy and obey the voice of God. Feel free to share with others who are in ministry and those deeply considering their call on their life. This book is a "must read" for leaders and pastors.

Elder Geraldine Walton
Spiritual Mother, Chicago

A Special Prayer for the Readers of This Book

Father, I pray that those who read this book will allow the Holy Spirit to minister to them. Lord, I realize that many are called but few are chosen. I pray that the chosen will be enlightened, strengthened, encouraged and empowered to heed and obey your voice. I pray that God will be able to use every reader to reach the multitude, heal the sick, and bring deliverance. I pray that each leader will seek your face and have a personal intimate relationship with you dear Lord.

Lord, we thank God for our leaders who are sold out to you. Thank you for the leaders who will be blessed by this message to live the assignment that you have given them. I pray for those who hear your voice calling them and will answer "Here am I; Send me."

I'm praying that God will increase their insight, discernment, awareness, understanding, comprehension and gain greater revelation of your plan for their lives. Father, may you enlarge the vision and wisdom of every reader. I pray that every reader will hear, know and obey the voice of God. I pray that leaders and pastors will move forward in the ministry to the service for which they have been called them.

I thank you Lord in advance that this book will reach those you designed it to reach. I pray their life and ministry will never be the same.

Father, I thank you for the obedience of Evangelist Karen Harris to write and encourage our leaders and pastors today. Holy Spirit, I thank you for pouring deep into her heart to write this phenomenal book. I also thank you in advance for the many books that will come after this one.

My deepest prayer and glory to the most high God,

Elder Geraldine Walton

TABLE OF CONTENTS

Chapter 1
Understand the Call

Chapter 2
What time is it?

Chapter 3
To die or not to die

Chapter 4
To see his Glory

Chapter 5
The Woe experience

Chapter 6
A Purge Cleansing

Chapter 7
Knowing God's voice

Chapter 8
Moving at God's voice

Chapter 9
The Unpopular word

Chapter 10
Calling Fulfilled

Introduction

You are up one late night simply reading and studying the word of God. It may be early in the morning in your daily devotion with God. Something is different this time. You hear a clear voice calling you for service. You are not sure what is happening but you hear it again. Day after day you hear the voice in your head. Everywhere you turn you see or hear something that confirms the voice you heard. The voice will not leave your head. It follows you. You try to disregard the voice. After months of ignoring the voice, you finally give up and say to the Lord, Here am I; send me. It's hard for you to understand why God chose you. You feel unfit, inadequate and not qualified for the job. Who am I, you ask yourself?

It is my goal that you will walk away with a clear understanding of your calling and the enormous responsibility and the magnitude of the call. God requires high standards from his leaders and pastors because he has entrusted us with a great responsibility. You will be able to evaluate or re-evaluate your life to make sure you are on the right path in fulfilling what God has placed in your heart. It is my hope that your life, calling and ministry will shift and take you to unbelievable places.

The calling to God's ministry can be scary, frightening and overwhelming at first. Anything we do for God is a great work. This book is intended to provoke us to carefully and seriously consider this great calling before moving forward in any type of ministry. The Word of God is our roadmap. God is looking for us to serve with a willing heart. The call to God's ministry requires three things according to Ephesians 4:12, perfecting of the saints, for the work of the ministry and edifying the body of Christ. Answering God's call to ministry is not to be taken lightly. When I was called to ministry I sought God intensely. I was fully aware of the seriousness of the calling. God is looking for powerful leaders to answer his call.

Chapter 1

UNDERSTAND THE CALL

Isaiah 6:8

Also I heard the voice of the Lord, saying whom shall I send and who will go for us? Then said I, Here am I; send me.

When we hear this scripture quoted or preached we get excited, raise our hands, and jump in agreement by declaring, yes! Lord, send me, I'll go! It has to become more than a quick slogan for a high powered service. We must stop to reflect, do we really **understand the call?**

It is not a call to go to the mall or a movie theatre. It is not a call to go on a vacation or to a ball game. It is not a call to have an entourage of armor bearers walking behind us. It is not a call for someone to carry our Bible and wait on us hand and foot. This call is a beautiful precious gift. The Bible states in *Romans 10:15 ...As it is written, How beautiful are the feet of them that preach the gospel of peace, and bring glad tidings of good things!* This call is to be treasured and honored. This call is not easily answered or accepted, *Matthew 22:14 For many are called, but few are chosen*. This call will change our life. This call may cause us to walk alone. This call will cause us to lose some friends.

There was a young man in the Bible who was wealthy. He asked Jesus what he must do to gain eternal life. Jesus gave him a list of things and the young man responded "I have kept all these things." Jesus told him in *Matthew 19:21-22 If thou wilt be perfect, go and sell that thou hast, and thou shalt have treasure in heaven: and come and follow me. But the young man heard that saying, he went away sorrowful: for he had great possessions.* Jesus called for this young man to follow him. The young man could not give up his treasured possessions to follow Christ. There is a cost attached to answering the call. We have to understand the call. What will the call require us to do? These questions have to be answered before we respond.

I have few questions I ask anyone who says they have been called to God's ministry. Why do you want to go? And go where? Are you ready to go? Can God trust you to go? Just because we have a call to God's ministry does not mean it is necessarily a call to go into a pulpit. We may operate from the streets, from a shelter home or hospital. What do you hear? Do you hear a call to be an evangelist, pastor, teacher, prophet, or apostle? Do you hear a call to be a worship leader, to work in the hospitality field or prison ministry? Do you hear a call to be a prayer warrior or intercessor? Has God called you to exhort the people? **Understand the call.**

In verse 8 of Isaiah 6, Isaiah understood the call and was ready and prepared to go. Are you ready and prepared to go? Are you ready to do whatever the Holy Spirit leads you to do or leads you to go? Are you ready to preach in season and out of season? Are you ready to preach when it's popular and when it's not? Paul teaches in *2 Timothy 4:2 Preach the word; be instant in season, out of season; reprove, rebuke, exhort with all long suffering and doctrine.* Isaiah was not called to an exciting or joyous mission. *Isaiah 6:10-12 Make the heart of this people fat, and make their ears heavy, and shut their eyes: lest they see with their eyes, and hear with their ears, and understand with their heart, and convert, and be healed. Then said I, Lord, how long?*

And he answered, Until the cities be wasted without inhabitant, and the house without man, and the land be utterly desolate, And the Lord have removed men far away, and there be a great forsaking in the midst of the land. Have we thought about the type of call Isaiah was called to? Have we thought about preaching today's unpopular message on holy and righteous living? Have we thought about having to rebuke or preach against sin? Are we ready to preach truth to people of hardened hearts and deaf ears? This is what Isaiah answered, here am I, send me.

Understand the call.

Being called to preach the gospel is more than preaching a sermon in a pulpit on a Sunday morning. When I was in college I had a close relationship with the local seminary school. Many of the students dreamed of building a mega church with thousands of members. I was listening for those who wanted to change lives or make a difference in the community. I was looking for leaders whose lifestyles lined up with God's word. Our calling is impactful when it mirrors the calling of Jesus Christ. Jesus was called to save the lost. As Jesus walked out His ministry, He taught, healed, delivered and set the captives free. This part of the call is very important. We add to the call an intense desire to serve. Jesus left us the greatest illustration of service as he served his disciples by washing their feet. *John 13:5-8 After that he poureth water into a basin, and began to wash the disciples' feet, and to wipe them with the towel wherewith he was girded. Then cometh he to Simon Peter: and Peter saith unto him, Lord, dost thou wash my feet? Jesus answered and said unto him, what I do thou knowest not now: but thou shalt know hereafter. Peter saith unto him, Thou shalt never wash my feet. Jesus answered him, if I wash thee not, thou hast no part with me.*

Are you ready to serve? How far are you willing to go to serve? We are seeing a growing generation of leaders, preachers and pastors who desire to be served vs. serving others. Simon Peter did not understand this teaching. In Peter's mind he felt that he was not worthy to allow Jesus, the Savior of the world, to wash his feet. Jesus was teaching his disciples a powerful leadership lesson. Jesus demonstrated to his disciples that being the Christ, the Savior, healer, deliverer, and redeemer did not stop him from serving others. Before he died, Jesus chose to serve. He knelt down and washed their feet. His model behavior shows us how important service is in the life of a leader.

I get excited when I see pastors and leaders sit and mingle with their congregation. I enjoy seeing our leaders show love and render service. This experience keeps us humble. As leaders, we are to watch our special benefits and privileges. Pride has a way of creeping in if we are not careful. Jesus demonstrated humility when he rode into Jerusalem on a donkey. Jesus lived to serve not to be served. Jesus made it very clear to Peter that it was important for his feet to be washed by his leader. I believe Christ was saying we are to be willing to serve the poor, the sick, the lost, and those who are in despair.

It's important to consider the cost of ministry as we heed the voice of Christ. *Luke 14:28 For which of you, intending to build a tower sitteth not down first, and counteth the cost whether he have sufficient to finish it?* As we know, it is easy to start a ministry or launch a business. Our challenge is to finish well. Before we decide to start a ministry or pastor a church, we have to consider the requirements of the call. *Luke 12:48b For unto whomsoever much is given, of him shall be much required: and to whom men have committed much, of him they will ask the more.* Jesus told a powerful parable that illustrates this lesson in Matthew 25. The business owner is going out of town and gave his servants responsibilities to perform while he was away. He gave them talents according to their abilities. One servant was given five talents. One was given two talents. The third servant was given one talent. The master expected more from the servant who was given five talents. At the master's return, we see that the servant with five talents earned five more talents. Much was given to him and much was expected of him. God requires much from us even today.

God not only expects much from the gifts and talents he put in us, but he also requires a life of purity. We must examine our personal relationship with God on a daily basis. How much time do we spend in prayer and in His presence? How much time are we investing in reading the Word of God? Are we studying God's Word only to deliver a message on Sunday morning?

Are we studying God's Word so that He can minister to us and impart revelations for our lives? What does our private lives look like? Do we have patience? Are we easily frustrated or angered? Are we kind and nice? Do we walk in the fruit of the spirit of love, meekness, kindness, patience, temperance, longsuffering, and gentleness? Are we ready to start our journey of faith? Do we have strongholds in our life? Are we engaging in sinful habits in our life? Do we have unforgiveness in our heart? What does our social life look like? What type of company do we keep? Do we gossip? Do we have ungodly conversations?

These are important questions to answer. These issues will arise in our teaching and preaching. How can we effectively teach against such things that are currently in our own lives? Jesus posed a question to his disciples in Luke 6:39 can the blind lead the blind? Jesus continued to say to his disciples, *And why beholdest thou the mote that is in thy brother's eye, but perceivest not the beam that is in thine own eye? Either how canst thou say to thy brother, Brother, let me pull out the mote that is in thine eye, when thou thyself beholdest not the beam that is in thine own eye? Thou hypocrite, cast out first the beam out of thine own eye, and then shalt thou see clearly to pull out the mote that is in thy brother's eye. Luke 6:41-42.*

In considering the cost of our call we have to consider and understand the potential attacks on our life both naturally and spiritually. When we operate as God desires, we will create change in someone's life for the better. If people are accepting Jesus Christ as their savior, habits are broken, deliverances are occurring, minds are renewed, and hearts are changing. This mission will create a problem for Satan. Satan comes to steal, kill and destroy (John 10:10) as many people as possible. Our call will interfere with Satan's plan. Satan will work hard to distract us, put obstacles in our way, and attack our minds to stop us. Satan tried several times to stop the birth and ministry of Christ. Satan used King Herod to try to kill Jesus as a baby (Matthew 2:16). In Matthew 4, Satan himself tried to stop Jesus' assignment by tempting him in the wilderness and then again on a high mountain. Fear not. *Isaiah 54:17 No weapon that is formed against thee shall prosper; and every tongue that shall rise against thee in judgment thou shalt condemn. This is the heritage of the servants of the Lord, and their righteousness is of me, saith the Lord.* Satan may throw obstacles our way. We are not to be afraid. We can trust *Psalm 91:1 He that dwelleth in the secret place of the most high shall abide under the shadow of the almighty.* There is protection in the will of God. I cannot stress enough how important it is to know our calling, understand the true work of the calling and have a personal relationship with Christ. **Understand the call.**

Is it time to go forward in our ministry? Are we stepping out before our time? Have we allowed God to prepare us, mold us and make us mighty for the call? Even Jesus did not launch his ministry immediately after being called. Jesus was called to leave heaven, came to earth by way of a virgin and then was prepared for his ministry that would begin 30 years later. Although Jesus obeyed his mother when he turned water into wine, he told her it was not his time, *John 2:4 Jesus saith unto her, Woman, what have I to do with thee? Mine hour is not yet come.*

To be called to God's ministry is more than the call itself. We are to know what the call means for us. We must know to whom we have we been called. Jesus is our prime example. Jesus understood that his call was to die for others. In order for him to die for others he had to first die to his will and do the will of His Father. Jesus spoke these powerful words to his Father in the Garden of Gethsemane? *Luke 22:42 Saying, Father, if thou be willing, remove this cup from me: nevertheless not my will, but thine, be done.* Are we ready to die to ourselves, our desires, and dreams for the sake of Christ and our assignment to others? Take a few minutes and let's think on this. If we cannot say for certain, Lord not my will but thine will be done in me, we may not be ready or prepared to say "Here am I; send me". Let me share an experience with you. A few years ago I was washing dishes in my kitchen. I was worshipping and thinking of the goodness of the Lord. Tears began to swell in my eyes. The presence of God was strong in my kitchen. At that moment I said to God I totally surrender my life to you. I knew exactly what that meant. It was no longer my desires but God's will for my life. If it meant I would not get the big house on the hill with a white picket fence, so be it. If it meant not driving my dream car, so be it. I realized at that moment I wanted what God planned for me. It was not an easy decision. What are we willing to give up for the call?

When Jesus called for the two fishermen, they immediately left their secular careers. *Matthew 4:18-19 And Jesus, walking by the Sea of Galilee, saw two brothers, Simon called Peter and Andrew his brother, casting a net into the sea; for they were fishers. And he saith unto them follow me and I will make you fishers of men. And they straightway left their nets and followed him.* Are we ready to forsake our goals and dreams for the call? I remember hearing a prominent prophet say that it was his dream to become a surgeon. He learned that becoming a surgeon was not God's will for his life. God called him to the nations as a prophet. He put away his own dreams and desires and followed the Lord's plan for his life. **Understand the call.**

We are beginning to see how important it is to truly understand the call. This call is not to be taken lightly. It's not to be used for personal gain. When we walk in our own desires and not God's desire we are walking on very dangerous grounds. Jesus himself said in *Matthew 7:22-23 Many will say to me in that day, Lord, Lord, have we not prophesied in thy name? And in thy name have cast out devils? And in thy name done many wonderful works? And then will I profess unto them, I never knew you: depart from me, ye that work iniquity.* God will allow us to use our gifts and talents and still miss the mark. He allows our gift to reach others. Yet we have to guard our hearts against iniquity at all times. Our call is to serve others.

It's powerful to know that God does not require us to be perfect to answer his call. The Bible is clear in *Romans 3:10 As it is written, There is none righteous, no, not one.* What makes us perfect is not the fact that we will never commit a sin or always do or say what is right. God looks at the intent of our heart. What's in our heart will be displayed outwardly. If our heart is pure God will be pleased with us. If we see our life as a set of rules and regulations, it will be difficult for us to experience the true love of Christ. As our relationship grows and our heart becomes mingled with Christ's heart, it no longer becomes a matter of rules or regulations. God's desires become our desires. If we fall into sin, it will grieve us to our core. It is not easy to sin when we have this type of relationship with Christ. It is at this point in our walk with Christ that every area of our life wants to please God. Hopefully, we will not find ourselves wrestling with sin. Thank God for his word, *1 John 1:9 if we confess our sins, he is faithful and just to forgive us our sins, and cleanse us from all unrighteousness.*

Thank God that our eyes are being opened to the importance of the call before launching our ministries. It is dangerous both physically and spiritually to move into ministry if our life is not representing Christ. We may also cause others to stumble in their faith. *Romans 14:13 Let us not therefore judge one another anymore: but judge this rather, that no man put a stumbling block or an occasion to fall in his brother's way.* The lifestyle of many leaders has caused many to fall and stumble, leave the church or lose hope in God. God holds us accountable for those souls. *James 3:1 Dear brothers and sisters, not many of you should become teachers in the church, for we who teach will be judged more strictly* (NLT). Eli's sons, Phinehas and Hophni were priests and they suffered the consequence of their actions. They mishandled the sacrifices and died.

When we understand the call and expectation of walking out the call, we will experience something beautiful. Paul said in *1 Timothy 3:1 This is a true saying, if a man desires the office of a bishop, he desireth a* good work. It is honorable to carry the gospel of Jesus Christ. We receive great gratification in serving others. It brings joy to our heart to see people healed from sickness and diseases and free from strongholds and habits. When we see lives changed because of the call on our life, we are humbled. It strengthens our faith to know God even more. Our feet are beautiful when we carry the gospel. **Let's understand the call.**

Chapter 2

WHAT TIME IS IT?

Isaiah 6:1

In the year that King Uzziah died I saw also the Lord...

What is time? According to the mathematical definition, time is an observed phenomenon by means of which human beings sense and record changes in the environment and in the universe. Numerous standards have been set up, allowing us to coordinate events and, in general keep our lives running smoothly. In the year King Uzziah died, Isaiah saw the Lord. This information allows us to put this event on a time line. We can pinpoint exactly when this occurred. Why is it important to know when this event happened? According to our definition of time, we notice there was a change in the environment. Prior to King Uzziah's death the environment or atmosphere was entirely different. At the end of one era, God will raise up a new era to show he is shifting things and us to meet his agenda. It is important to note that a change or shifting was occurring spiritually first, then naturally.

This shift occurred at the death of King Uzziah in 740 BC. *Ecclesiastes 3:1 To everything there is a season, and a time to every purpose under the heaven.* This scripture clearly states there is a season and a purpose. God does not do things just for the sake of it, there is a purpose! From Genesis to Revelation, we see God's amazing purpose. We experience the "changing of guards." God is ushering in a new revelation, new direction or a new shift in the spiritual realm. From the time of King Uzziah's death to Isaiah's encounter, we witness a changing of the guards. It is imperative for us to know why we have to launch or move at God's timing. Our calling is for others, as we stated in Chapter 1. God has timed our lives to impact the life of others.

This timing, however, is according to God's purpose not our timing. Human interference can alter the timing of God! *Deuteronomy 1:2 There are eleven days' journey from Horeb by way of mount Seir unto Kadesh-barnea* (Canaan). It was God's will for the children of Israel to enter the Promised Land in eleven days. However, because of their interference with their mouths by murmuring and complaining, the timing was extended to forty years. Let's watch our mouth! It's important to note that the original group of travelers did not cross over. God allowed their offspring to enter the promised land. We can interfere with God's timing by causing a delay of our ministry or calling. We can totally miss God's plan for us if we are not careful.

In 2012 God gave me the name for his ministry. Since he gave me the name I thought it was time to move forward. When I prepared to launch my ministry, I had received the name. Yet no doors opened. I realized that it was not time for me to move forward. If I had continued and tried to force the ministry to start in 2012, I believe I could have killed the ministry. Daniel wanted to understand his dream about the end times. God told him to not worry because the manifestation of the dream was way in the future. *Daniel 12:8-9 And I heard, but I understood not: then said I, O my Lord, what shall be the end of these things? And he said, Go thy way Daniel: for the words are closed up and sealed till the time of the end.* God revealed portions of the dream to

Daniel, but it was not time for the event to occur. David was chosen and anointed at 15 to be the next king of Israel. It took 15 years for the dream to be manifested. God may reveal to us our ministry or parts of our ministry, but it does not always mean it is time to launch.

Why would God reveal a calling that takes years to manifest? The same way a 5 year old child dreams of being a police officer. Would we give that child a badge and a gun because he dreams of being a police officer? Of course not. In every dream or calling there is a time of preparation. After Paul's encounter and conversion on the Damascus road he did not start preaching immediately. According to Biblical scholars his ministry or missionary journeys started about ten years later. It is believed that Paul went through a time of preparation. *Galatians 1:12 I received my message from no human source, and no one taught me. Instead, I received it by direct revelation from Jesus Christ* (NLT). During our time of preparation, God will teach us through different ways--directly from the Word, prayer, personal time with God, a preached word from our pastor, and through life experiences. He will use challenges that will strengthen our faith in God. During my time of preparation, from the time I heard the call until now, I grew spiritually by leaps and bounds. My personal preparation time before launching the ministry he gave me was sixteen years. That may seem like a long time. I have to admit there were times when I became weary but God strengthened me to trust him and allow him to work in me. Preparation time will vary from person to person. God has a set time for us and we have to trust him. We cannot answer why God allows one to be in preparation for one to two years and another like myself for sixteen years. We just have to trust God.

If we are not ready God may allow us to move forward because we can override him. Forcing the move may damage us and others. The children of Israel were not ready to be in the Promised Land in eleven days so they had to wait forty years. A few years ago I had a very clear vivid dream. In this dream I was waiting backstage in a large coliseum that was packed with people waiting on me to preach God's word. As I was standing backstage I was nervously flipping through the pages of the Bible trying to find something to preach. At that moment I woke up confused. I asked the Lord what the dream meant. Immediately he answered, "you are not ready." I cried deeply and asked God for forgiveness for my laziness and slothfulness in my personal spiritual growth. Was my timing delayed because of my own actions? Possibly, but I cannot say for certain.

I committed myself to studying God's word more, praying more, entering his presence more which allowed me to know him more and begin to hear his voice clearly. I used the time of preparation to serve in my local church and whatever else the Lord instructed me to do. As a result of committed time my heart grew tremendously with the love of Jesus Christ.

What time is it? Is it time to launch or is this the time of preparation? How do we know what time period we are in? If you are not sure if it's a time of preparing most likely it is not time to launch. It is vital that we are able to hear the voice of God concerning when to launch our ministry and hear instructions. Moving too fast or before God tells us may cause our ministry to be crippled, dysfunctional and possibly die before it starts. I realized through my own personal experience that in order to lead God's people, we have to hear his voice and know it's his voice. Satan has a voice too that will lie to us. God called for Samuel three times. Samuel did not have the experience to recognize God's voice. Eli had to help Samuel recognize the voice of God (1 Samuel 3:4-9). In verse seven, we see that Samuel did not know the Lord and this is why he did not recognize his voice. We have to know God to know his voice. If we are struggling to know his voice, we need to begin to spend personal intimate time in the presence of God. The closer we get to God we will begin to hear his voice and instructions for our ministry. In order to get to that place we have to seek him diligently. *Matthew 7:7-8 Ask, and it shall be given you: seek, and ye shall find; knock, and it shall be opened unto you. For everyone that asketh receiveth, and he seeketh findeth; and to him that knocketh it shall be opened.* These scriptures speak of a deep intimate personal relationship with God. This involves seeking God intently and intensely until he is found. *Isaiah 45:15 Verily thou art a God that hidest thyself, O God of Israel the Saviour.* God will hide himself to see how much we desire him. God pulled away and hid from Hezekiah to find out what was in his heart (2 Chronicles 32:31). People who desire to be a medical doctor spend insurmountable hours studying in order to become a physician. How much time are we willing to spend with God for that amazing relationship? Our relationship with God is directly connected to the success of our ministry.

The year King Uzziah died speaks of two times; when it occurred on a timeline and a time of change, shifting and launching. For Isaiah, it was a shifting in his life. His experience propelled him to answer by saying "Here am I; send me." Isaiah was in the right place at the right time. We've talked about making sure we avoid a premature launch.

Let's explore the other side of the ministry equation. Can we miss our time? There are several reasons why we can miss our time. Our top culprits are murmuring, complaining, laziness, slothfulness, fear, sin and distractions. The children of Israel missed their time of entering the Promised Land because they murmured and complained. Our mouth will cause us to miss our time. Our tongue is a powerful tool. If we better understood how the tongue can create life, we would pay more attention to the things we say. *Proverbs 18:21 Death and life are in the power of the tongue: and they that love it shall eat the fruit thereof.* Gossiping and having ungodly conversations about others will also cause us to miss our time. *1 Peter 3:10 For he that will love life, and see good days, let him refrain his tongue from evil, and his lips that they speak no guile. Ephesians 4:29 Let no corrupt communication proceed out of your mouth, but that which is good to the use of edifying, that it may minister grace unto the hearers.*

There are many scriptures about the tongue. I encourage you to read and study the following scriptures: Proverbs 10:19, James 3:6, Psalm 19:14, Proverbs 15:4 and Proverbs 13:3. Let's use our tongue to speak life, encouragement and hope. We will edify others.

Secondly, laziness and slothfulness are robbers of destiny. Moving slow can cause us to miss our time. The Bible is very clear regarding this. *Proverbs 10:4 He becometh poor that dealeth with a slack hand: but the hand of the diligent maketh rich.* Also, *Proverbs 13:4 The soul of the sluggard desireth, and hath nothing: but the soul of the diligent shall be made fat.* In primary school the teacher asked the class to write a paragraph on what we wanted to be when we grew up. We have dreams and aspirations as a young child of what we want to do in life. It takes diligent efforts to make our dreams come true. I suffer in the areas of laziness and procrastination. I pray often for the strength to do what I need to do when it needs to be done. What has helped me to overcome this weakness is to have an organized and structured life. The servant that was given one talent was dealing with slothfulness. He buried his talent and did not produce more. *Matthew 25:26 His lord answered and said unto him, Thou wicked and slothful servant, thou knewest that I reap where I sowed not, and gather where I have not strawed.* I know people today with great gifts and talents who are not moving forward because of slothfulness. It takes a made up mind, dedication and hard work to accomplish any goals that we may have. Even as I write this book, I have spent many hours writing and researching.

This takes commitment. The end result is well worth the sweat and tears. What if Joshua was tired and lazy and did not complete the march around Jericho seven times as God instructed? We know the walls would have never fallen.

Fear is possibly the greatest way to miss our calling. Fear can cripple us and keep us from moving forward. Fear of failure has stopped leaders from pursuing their call or the gift that God has placed in them. Fear is one of Satan's greatest weapons; he uses fear strategically so we stop achieving God's plan. Satan is the source of fear. How do we overcome fear? We get to know God's perfect love towards us. *1 John 4:18 There is no fear in love: but perfect love casteth out fear: because fear hath torment. He that feareth is not made perfect in love.* We have to know the love of God for us in order to cast out fear. For years I feared for my children. My daughter Mariah is allergic to peanuts and shellfish. She also has asthma. My son Keenan has experienced several attacks in his body and was involved in accidents.

When my children would call me at work, I would panic before I answered the phone. I would see their number and become very anxious wondering what was wrong. The Lord impressed it on my heart to study God's love. As I continued to study, God's love began to grow deeper in my own heart. The love of God grew stronger in my life. When I thought of his love I would weep. Studying God's incredible love made me realize that my children were under the protection of the almighty God. Now when my children call, I am no longer afraid to answer the phone. Knowing the love of God has given me power and authority to cast out my fear! *2 Timothy 1:7 For God has not given us a spirit of fear, but of power and of love and of a sound mind.*

Not only do we have power to cast out fear but we have power and authority over serpents and scorpions. *Luke 10:19 Behold, I give unto you power to tread on serpents and scorpions, and over all the power to the enemy: and nothing shall by any means hurt you.* Knowing who we are in Christ Jesus will empower us to trample the enemy. Fear can cause anxiety, panic attacks, depression, suicidal ideation and much more. Fear is a great weapon for Satan. He uses it so that we walk afraid and miss our time.

Another major cause for missing our time is SIN. Sin disconnects us from God. If we are disconnected we cannot hear his voice for instructions or directions. God does not hear our prayers when we walk in sin. *John 9:31 Now we know that God heareth not sinners: but if a man be a worshipper of God, and doeth his will, him he heareth.* Sin is a stench in God's nostrils and a smell that never goes away (Isaiah 65:5). First, let's be clear and understand that all have sinned and come short of God's glory (Romans 3:23). We may fall into sin because we are not perfect. In these cases we have a gracious Father who is just and faithful to forgive us and cleanse us from all unrighteousness (1 John 1:9).

It is practicing a life of sin that will detour us from moving forward in God's calling. What do I mean? A life of sin is practiced on a daily or consistent basis. Our mouth may say we love God but our heart is far from him. *Matthew 15:8 This people draweth nigh unto me with their mouth, and honoureth me with their lips; but their heart is far from me. John 14:15 If ye love me, keep my commandments.* Sin caused the children of Israel to suffer many things; captivity, famine, poverty, and death to name a few. When they obeyed the word of the Lord blessings flowed like milk and honey. Let's not allow sin to cause us to miss our time. When you are really in Christ Jesus we will not want to live in sin. I have heard plenty of these excuses. We are human. God knows my heart. Don't judge me. Although these responses are true, we can use them as excuses for not living a holy life. There are numerous scriptures that show us we can live a life free of sin. *1 Peter 3:15-16 But as he which hath called you is holy, so be ye holy in all manner of conversation. Because it is written, Be ye holy; for I am holy. Philippians 4:13 I can do all things through Christ which strengthened me.* The key word in the scripture is strengthen. It is difficult to be strengthened if we do not have a personal relationship with Christ. We will be weak if we do not seek his face on a consistent basis by spending time in his presence. In this case our flesh is dominating our spirit. *Galatians 5:24 Those who belong to Christ Jesus have nailed the passions and desires of their sinful nature to his cross and crucified them there (NLT).* Our heart will follow our treasure (Matthew 6:21).

Distraction will cause us to miss our time. It is important that we stay focused. The world presents us with so many distractions. Distraction from our children, spouse, career, television, social media, telephone and more. We are distracted when our eyes are not focused on God. Remember God called Peter to walk on water. Peter was fulfilling that call until he was distracted by the raging storm. Peter began to sink because his eyes were no longer focused on Jesus who was training him to walk on the water. (Matthew 14:29-30). If we stay steadfast, unmovable and always abounding in the work of the Lord (1 Corinthians 15:58), we will stay focused. Staying in God's word keeps us focused on our mission. *Joshua 1:8 This book of the law shall not depart out of thy mouth; but thou shalt meditate therein day and night, that thou mayest observe to do according to all that is written therein: for then thou shalt make thy way prosperous, and thou shalt have good success.* The latter portion of this verse clearly states that we will be prosperous and have good success when we keep our eyes on God. Horses wear blinders. Horse blinders are leather squares cups that are attached to a horse's bridle. The blinders prevent a horse from seeing in any direction but straight ahead. Horses that pull wagons and carriages wear blinders to prevent them from becoming distracted or panicked by what they see behind the wagon. Let's go back to Peter, because he did not have on his spiritual blinders. He was fearful of the raging waters and blowing winds. He panicked and believed he was going to drown. We, too, have to put on spiritual blinders to keep us focused on our calling and the time to launch.

We are all put on this earth for a purpose. I have heard many people say once they have reached a certain age that they wished they would have done more. Many people have departed from this earth unfulfilled. They did not live out the plan God had for them. *John 9:4 I must work the works of him that sent me, while it is day: the night cometh, when no man can work.* Are you living God's will for your life? Time on earth does not stop. The clock continues to tick whether we live our calling or not. How many times have we said, "time flies" or "where did time go?" I encouraged a few of the young ladies that I work with to go back to school for higher degrees. I saw great potential in them. Years later many have not made it to school and are still making the same amount of money. Their comments are "I could have been done by now." If we do not move when the spirit of God touches us, we will regret it later. Time waits for no man. Even God after a while will go to the next willing vessel because his agenda has to be fulfilled through us or someone else. *Ecclesiastes 3:2 A time to be born, and a time to die; a time to plant, and a time to pluck up that which is planted.* There is a set time for our ministry to be born and harvested. Let's not miss our time. Let's redeem it! We can get started today and work diligently to make up for time wasted.

Chapter 3

TO DIE OR NOT TO DIE

Isaiah 6:1

In the year that king Uzziah died...

King Uzziah experienced two deaths, a spiritual death and a natural death. King Uzziah is an example of many kings in the Bible as well as many ministers and leaders today. We start out doing the will of God but along the way we were side tracked and turn away from the things of God. King Uzziah became king at sixteen and reigned for fifty two years. He had great success. He did everything that was right in the sight of the Lord. God gave him success to conquer many nations. He built many towers and a strong army. As long as King Uzziah sought the Lord, God made him to prosper. As King Uzziah's popularity grew and because of his great success he began to die spiritually by being lifted up in pride. *2 Chronicles 26:16 But when he was strong, his heart was lifted up to his destruction: for he transgressed against the Lord his God, and went into the temple of the Lord to burn incense upon the altar of incense.* It was a sin for anyone but the chosen priests to go in the holy area of the temple and burn incense. The priests tried to stop King Uzziah but he would not listen. He became angry at them. God struck King Uzziah with leprosy for the remainder of his life. It is important to know King Uzziah became prideful before he fell into sin. *Proverbs 16:18 Pride goeth before destruction, and a haughty spirit before a fall.* The result of pride is that we think we can do what we desire. We believe that nothing will happen to us. King Uzziah first died spiritually and then naturally.

Anytime we move from God's will to our own agenda, we are in danger of dying spiritually. King Saul disobeyed God's instructions which led to his spiritual death and the spirit of the Lord departed from him. The spirit of the Lord departed from Saul but he remained king for many more years. Saul reigned for forty two years. Saul was dead spiritually during his reign but remained in power physically as king over Israel. We can be dead spiritually but remain in power as pastor or leader. Why does God allow this to happen? God will allow our gifts or talents to still operate because our gift is for others and not ourselves. This dynamic puts the leader in a dangerous position. We can start off with God and then fall away? It does not happen abruptly. It happens gradually and subtly until the person does not even realize what is taking place. In the Garden of Eden the serpent deceived Eve. The serpent came to Eve very subtly. She was not aware of his true intent. He disguised his motive and invited her to doubt God. He is shrewd. Satan starts in a small way. For example, a pastor who is busy running his ministry may begin to neglect his private time with God. He loves performing the activities of the ministry more than spending time with God who gave him the ministry. Whenever our intimate time with God begins to decrease, our discernment also decreases. We are connected to the spiritual things by staying connecting with God in prayer and lingering in his presence.

King Uzziah's spiritual death ultimately led to his natural death. As King Uzziah began to become prideful in his heart, he began to die spiritually. He sinned against God and died a natural death. God hates a proud heart. *Proverbs 16:5 Every one that is proud in heart is an abomination to the Lord: though hand join in hand, he shall not be unpunished.* King Uzziah sinned against God by going into the temple after his heart was lifted up in pride. He was struck with leprosy while still in the temple. Sin can cause sickness in your body and eventually death. *Psalm 107:17-18 Fools, because of their transgression, and because of their iniquities, are afflicted. Their soul abhorreth all manner of meat: and they draw near unto the gates of death.* I have seen patients near death have no desire for food. King Uzziah was struck with leprosy when the priests warned him not to burn incense in the temple. God will warn us before we fall. God warned the children of Israel of what would happen if they continued in their sins. God used Jeremiah to warn Judah of judgment and destruction before it came. *Jeremiah 6:10 To whom can I speak and give warning? Who will listen to me? Their ears are closed so they cannot hear. The word of the Lord is offensive to them; they find no pleasure in it.* (NIV)

King Uzziah chose to die spiritually instead of dying to his flesh. He did not have to die early. We can choose to die to the desires of our flesh and live. *Joshua 24:15 And if it seem evil unto you to serve the Lord, choose you this day whom ye will serve; whether the gods which your fathers served that were on the other side of the flood, or the gods of the Amorites, in whose land ye dwell: but as for me and my house, we will serve the Lord.* It is impossible to live for God and the world. The Bible states that we will love one and hate the other. *Matthew 6:24 No one can serve two masters. For you will hate one and love the other; you will be devoted to one and despise the other. You cannot serve both God and money.* This scripture proves true every day as we continue to see great men fall from God to their fleshly desires. We are not able to please both our flesh and serve in God's ministry. We will fall spiritually and our ministries will suffer when we do not deny our flesh. *Galatians 5:24 And they that are Christ's have crucified the flesh with the affections and lusts.*

In Romans Paul teaches extensively on the topic of being free from sin and our fleshly desires. In the 7th chapter of Romans, Paul speaks of the agony and frustration of being torn between our fleshly desires and our desire to please God. He explains that there is a war going on in our members. Good vs. evil. *Romans 7:20-23 Now if I do that I would not, it is no more I that do it, but sin that dwelleth in me. I find then a law, that, when I would do good, evil is present with me. For I delight in the law of God after the inward man: But I see another law in my members, warring against the law of my mind, and bringing me into captivity to the law of sin which is in my members.* This is not an excuse to sin. While we may have a battle, we must let righteousness reign over sin. Fight back with faith and fortitude. In the entire 7th chapter of Romans, Paul is describing a spiritual tug-of-war in pleasing God. In this sport, the opponents pull back and forth until finally the winner gains the advantage. We as Christians have the home court advantage. Christ has already won the battle against our enemy. Romans 7: 20-23 declares *O wretched man that I am! Who shall deliver me from the body of this death? I thank God through Jesus Christ our Lord.*

Satan has deceived many by causing them to think the pleasure of the flesh is better than the pleasures of following Christ wholeheartedly. King Uzziah appeared to have it all. He was successful and prosperous because he followed the way of God. Satan shot a dart laced with fleshly pride. King Uzziah did not put the dart's fire out. He let it burn him and destroy his successful reign. Satan enjoys capturing the hearts of kings. He had the audacity to approach the King of Kings. Satan promised Jesus a world that he already owned. Jesus snuffed out the fiery dart of pride. *Matthew 4:8-9 Again, the devil taketh him up into an exceeding high mountain, and sheweth him all the kingdoms of the world, and the glory of them; And saith unto him, All these things will I give thee, if thou wilt fall down and worship me.* Satan wanted Christ to worship him. How could Satan offer Christ what already belonged to him? Satan is cunning and sneaky. Yet, Christ was fully convinced of living a righteous life. We can be too. Romans 7:25 in its entirety says, *I thank God through Jesus Christ our Lord. So then with the mind I myself serve the law of the God; but with the flesh the law of sin.* Our flesh will always work contrary to the word of God. Renewing our minds daily will overcome our flesh. If our mind is renewed consistently in Christ, our spirit man will reign supreme. A strong spirit man will overcome our temptations. *Romans 12:2 And be not conformed to this world: but be ye transformed by the renewing of your mind, that ye may prove what is that good, and acceptable, and perfect, will of God.* We will be transformed to walk in righteousness while still living in our flesh.

Once King Uzziah sinned he was struck with leprosy. Due to the infectious nature of leprosy, king Uzziah had to be removed from leading and was put in isolation for the remaining of his life. If we allow Satan to take control of our life, we too will be removed and isolated from God. Leaders who refused to die to the lust of their flesh lost their ministries and watched a more worthy leader oversee their church. King Uzziah did not make it back to his throne; his son Jotham replaced him as king. Thanks be to God we can "come to ourselves" like the prodigal son did and come back home! (Luke 15:17) We can repent of our sins and stubbornness and come back to God. He is waiting with open arms.

Deciding to die to our flesh is will revitalize our spiritual life, natural life and our ministry. Our flesh is attracted to the glamour, lights, and camera. God will give us all of these desires if we guard our hearts and stay humble. We do not have to seek fame, fortune or material gain. God will add wealth if we make him first in our lives... *Matthew 6:33 But seek ye first the kingdom of God, and his righteousness; and all these things shall be added unto you.* Solomon shows us how desiring to please God first resulted in an avalanche of blessings for his kingdom. *1 Kings 3:9-14 Give therefore thy servant an understanding heart to judge thy people, that I may discern between good and bad: for who is able to judge this thy so great a people? And the speech pleased the Lord, that Solomon had asked this thing. And God said unto him, Because thou hast asked this thing, and hast not asked for thyself long life; neither hast asked riches for thyself, nor hast asked the life of thine enemies; but hast asked for thyself understanding to discern judgment; Behold, I have done according to thy works: lo, I have given thee a wise and an understanding heart; so that there was none like thee before thee, neither after thee shall any arise like unto thee. And I have also given thee that which thou hast not asked, both riches, and honour: so that there shall not be any among the kings like unto thee all thy days. And if thou walk in my ways, to keep my statutes and my commandments, as thy father David did walk, then I will lengthen thy days.*

Solomon understood that his ministry was for others and not himself. I believe Solomon gripped the heart of God because of his sincerity to serve his chosen people. When we serve people we are serving God. He takes our efforts seriously, this is why he blessed and prospered Solomon. In Matthew 25 verse 40 Jesus lets us know how we treat his people is how we treat him *And the King will say, I tell you the truth, when you did it to one of the least of these my brothers and sisters, you were doing it to me!* (NLT).

When we choose to deny our flesh and die to the things of the world and serve God's people, blessing will overtake us. Solomon's life demonstrated God takes care of his leaders. Not only will we prosper here on earth, but we will also inherit the Kingdom. Jesus explains who will inherit the Kingdom and why. *Matthew 25:34 Then the King will say to those on his right, Come, you who are blessed by my Father, inherit the Kingdom prepared for you from the creation of the world. For I was hungry, and you fed me. I was thirsty, and you gave me a drink. I was a stranger, and you invited me into your home. I was naked, and you gave me clothing. I was sick, and you cared for me. I was in prison, and you visited me.* Notice that Jesus did not say because we preached with power we will inherit the Kingdom. He did not say running a mega church will cause us to inherit the Kingdom. He did not say popularity will cause us to inherit the Kingdom of God. We can have all these things and still perish. God is looking for those who will serve the least. Are we planning on having a prison ministry? Are we planning on going out into the community and serving the poor and feeding the hungry? God is looking for a ministry that will serve humanity.

Romans 6:23 For the wages of sin is death, but the gift of God is eternal life through Jesus Christ our Lord. The right death produces life and the wrong death produces death. Jesus' death produced life for those who will accept him. After salvation in Christ we experience death by water baptism. When we go down under the water our old life dies and when we emerge out of the watery grave our new life begins. We can expect a life of fruit and harvest, a life of joy and peace, and a life of blessings and abundance. A seed has to go through a death experience in order to sprout and bring forth a life of harvest. *John 12:24 Verily, verily, I say unto you except a corn of wheat fall into the ground and die, it abideth alone: but if it die, it bringeth forth much fruit.* As we walk out our calling, we are walking in the way of life. Sin separates us from God. *Isaiah 59:2 But your iniquities have separated between you and your God, and your sins have hid his face from you, that he will not hear.* This death can be an eternal death if we remain in our sins.

Which death will you choose? The death of Christ or the death of Satan. The cities of Sodom and Gomorrah were destroyed because they refused to repent of their sins. God destroyed many kings of the Old Testament because of their wickedness. King Rehoboam, King Ahab, King Ahaziah and King Manasseh just to name a few were wicked leaders of Israel and Judah. Leaders who live wicked lives can make their nations suffer. King Manasseh corrupted the nation of Judah. *2 Kings 23:26-27 Notwithstanding the Lord turned not from the fierceness of his great wrath, wherewith his anger was kindled against Judah, because of all the provocations that Manasseh had provoked him withal. And the Lord said, I will remove Judah also out of my sight, as I have removed Israel, and will cast off this city Jerusalem which I have said, My name shall be there.* A leader's spirit will flow to our followers. *Psalm 133:2 It is like the precious ointment upon the head, that ran down upon the beard, even Aaron's beard: that went down to the skirts of his garments.* This scripture speaks of a wonderful brotherly love when the saints come together. It is compared to oil that flows down from Aaron's beard to his garment. The oil will then flow to his followers.

Brotherly love is the same way. As we come together in our sanctuaries whatever is flowing from our pastor will flow down to us as members. If we have a loving and humble pastor, we will find a loving and humble congregation. If the leader is operating in a particular sin it will not be surprising to see the same sin in the congregation. Why? Because the spirit of that sin is flowing from the head (leader) to the body (members). This is why God holds us leaders more accountable than lay members. He has called us to be a watchman over his people. We are judged more strictly when we rise up to preach and lead people. As mentioned in Chapter 1 James *3:1 Dear brothers and sisters, not many of you should become teachers in the church, for we who teach will be judged more strictly* (NLT). Also worth mentioning again, *Luke 12:48b For unto whomsoever much is given, of him shall be much required.* Our life will affect those we are called to for better or for worse.

Our obedience or disobedience to God's instructions may cause the blood of our congregation to be on your hands. God warned Ezekiel that if he did not obey his word in giving a word warning, the person's blood will be on his hand. *Ezekiel 3:17-18 Son of man, I have made thee a watchman unto the house of Israel: therefore hear the word at my mouth, and give them warning from me. When I say unto the wicked, Thou shalt surely die; and thou givest him not warning, nor speakest to warn the wicked from his wicked way, to save his life; the same wicked man shall die in his iniquity; but his blood will I require at thine hand.* As we choose sermons and messages to bring to the congregation, we have to obey God. God may have us teach a message on a particular sin in order to bring correction. We have to die to what we want to preach and preach as the Holy Spirit directs.

When I knew for certain that God called me to ministry, I sought the Lord diligently. I said to God very seriously and sincerely "Lord, I cannot minister to anyone until you fix me and teach me." I knew how dangerous it is for pastors and leaders to lead God's people and be engaged in a life of sin. I do not want to live this kind of life. Why tempt God to destroy us by not dealing with the sins that cause us to stumble? Have we lost our fear and reverence for God? Because of this lack of fear many have operated knowingly in sin and suffered the consequences of their actions. *Hebrews 12:28-29 Wherefore we receiving a kingdom which cannot be moved, let us have grace, whereby we may serve God acceptably with reverence and godly fear: For our God is a consuming fire.* Aaron's sons were consumed by God's fire because of their sins. *Leviticus 10:1-2 And Nadab and Abihu the sons of Aaron, took either of them his censer, and put fire therein, and put incense thereon, and offered strange fire before the Lord, which he commanded them not. And there went out fire from the Lord, and devoured them, and they died before the Lord.* Why is God a consuming fire? His holiness causes him to be a consuming fire. God burns up unholy material. Who can withstand God's fire?

To die or not to die, it's our decision. Let's allow God to fully operate in our life. When God is captain and pilot of our life we will be amazed where he will take us. We have to make a decision to live in Christ. God will not make us do anything. God loves us so much. He wants us to willingly serve him. When we choose him freely it is from our heart. When we die to self, to our self-will and our selfish desires, our lives will be far better than we could ever imagine or dream. *Romans 8:13 For if ye live after the flesh, ye shall die: but if ye through the Spirit do mortify the deeds of the body, ye shall live.* Choose life in Christ Jesus.

Chapter 4

TO SEE GOD'S GLORY

Isaiah 6:1

In the year that king Uzziah died I saw the Lord sitting upon a throne, high and lifted up, and his train filled the temple.

An encounter with God will change our life forever. Isaiah's life was changed when he had a close encounter with God. What encounters have you had? What supernatural experiences have changed your life? I am convinced we cannot come in contact with the presence God and remain the same. It's impossible. Moses was forever changed when he came into the presence of God and saw the burning bush. Paul was forever changed when he supernaturally encountered Jesus on the road to Damascus. When we enter the presence of God, we never want to come out. In our heavenly Father's presence, we believers encounter so many wonderful experiences. There are mysteries God wants to reveal to us, but these hidden treasures are only found in his presence.

It's time for Christians to thirst after the treasures of God and experienced his glory. We may have never seen seraphim's like Isaiah or burning bushes like Moses, but God's glory shows up in many ways. God appears to mankind in various ways. To successfully operate in the ministry God has called us, we will desire to experience the presence of God regularly. Peace abides in his presence. His presence brings calmness when chaos is all around us. God's glory brings us beauty for ashes.

In God's presence we feel the beauty in him. God speaks to us and give us instructions. Assignments are missed when we are not in a place to hear God's voice. There are many other voices but the sheep knows the voice of his Shepherd. *John 10:27 My sheep hear my voice, and I know them, and they follow me.* God will speak in a small still voice. *1 Kings 19:12 And after the earthquake a fire: but the Lord was not in the fire: and after the fire a still small voice.* Every time I heard God's voice clearly I was always in a quiet place of worship or reading the word of God. We have to be positioned to hear God as leaders and pastors. What is God's plan for us and the people we lead? His presence keeps us nourished and transformed. When we have entered into God's presence, we have entered a sacred place. There is an expectation of a holy encounter for those who want to be in the presence of God and experience his glory.

We do not enter his presence like we enter a room. Entering into God's presence is like entering into the holy of holies of the tabernacle. When the priest entered the tabernacle he did not immediately enter the holy of holies. He first had to go through the outer court to the holy place and finally into the holy of holies. He could only enter the holy of holies one time a year. Today God is housed in our bodies. Now we can go in God's presence as often as we like. Holiness is a standard to enter his presence. He is our Lord of Lords and King of Kings.

We will use this tabernacle diagram as our example for entering in the presence of God and experiencing his glory. Every believer will need to know how to enter into God's presence. We will discover why so many Christians remain in the courtyard. The entire tabernacle structure is surrounded and enclosed by a gate of linen. Linen is a soft fabric. God desires us to come easily to him. Entering through the gate door represents thanksgiving. *Psalm 100:4 Enter into his gates with thanksgiving, and into his courts with praise: be thankful unto him, and bless his name.* We are designed to come through the gate with thanksgiving and to enter his courts with praise. This is the first step to entering the presence of God. We recognize that saying thank you is easy. We say thank you to people when they do something for us but that does not indicate we know them personally. We can enter the courtyard with much praise and thanksgiving; however, this outward expression is not an indicator of a deeper personal relationship experience with God. Keep moving. Inside the courtyard we see the brazen altar and laver. The brazen altar was made out of wood overlaid with bronze symbolizing suffering. Animals screamed in pain as they were being cut up to be sacrifices. The animals were to be used in our place. Instead of us being tied up and bound to be burned, the priests used animals for our sin offering. The brazen altar is a shadow of the suffering of Jesus Christ who too was sacrificed to redeem us from sin. The brazen altar had four horns in each corner. The horns were a place of safety. We see Biblical characters running into the temple and grabbing the horns as a way to escape death or seek asylum from their enemies who were pursuing them. *1 Kings 1:50 Adonijah feared because of Solomon, and arose, and went, and caught hold on the horns of the altar.*

Spiritually as we accept the sacrifice of Christ we also hold on to him (horns) for our forgiveness, our deliverance and die to our old life. Keep moving through the temple with me. In the courtyard just before the entrance way of the holy place is a laver. It is the sacred wash bowl of the tabernacle. God's servants were instructed to wash their hands and feet before they could enter the holy place. In the first tabernacle, the lavers were made from the metal mirrors the women brought out of Egypt (Exodus 38:8). The laver was made of pure bronze, the same material used by the women to see their reflections. The laver became our mirror to see ourselves as we became clean. Spiritually as we come closer to entering the presence of God we have to wash our hearts, minds and souls with word of God. God's word cleanses us through sanctification. When our lives are cleansed by the washing of God's word, our life should mirror the life of Christ. *James 1:23 For if any be a hearer of the word, and not a doer, he is like unto a man beholding his natural face in a glass: For he beholdeth himself, and goeth his way, and straightway forgetteth what manner of man he was. But whoso looketh into the perfect law of liberty, and continueth therein, he being not a forgetful hearer, but a doer of the work, this man shall be blessed in his deed.* In other words, we look into God's word for cleansing. The word allows us to see our reflection similar to looking in a mirror. When we look into a mirror, we discover what needs to be adjusted and changed before going out into the public. When we are purified by the word, we will see Christ. The priests could not enter into the holy place with dirty hands and feet. Likewise we cannot enter into the presence of God and be spiritually dirty. We must be cleansed by the laver. Washing our hands is something that we do. Unfortunately, many of us do not self cleanse and therefore we do not make it past the courtyard. Many believers want to experience a great manifestation from God in their life, but do not want to allow the word to cleanse our lives. As leaders, pastors, and those called to the fivefold ministry, it is a matter of life and death to study and know the word of God. Ministers who remain in the courtyard are not effective leaders. As you begin to read and study God's word for cleansing (washing our hands in the laver), something supernatural starts to take place. The spirit of God begins to take over. At this point you are entering the holy place. The tabernacle consists of two separate compartments, the holy place and the holy of holies. Unlike the courtyard area, the tabernacle ceiling is covered with four layers of skin. There is no light coming in. We are in total darkness in the holy place. In the holy place there is the table of showbread, the golden lampstand and the altar of incense. The table of showbread was made of wood overlaid with gold. On the table were twelve loaves of bread separated in two stacks of six representing the twelve tribes of Israel. The bread represents a food offering to God. Only Aaron and his sons (top leaders and pastors) were allowed to service the table the showbread.

The table of showbread is sometimes referred to the table of presence. It is in the holy place where we begin to experience the presence of God. At the laver just outside of the holy place, cleansing is taking place by the written word. As we are being cleansed the spirit of God takes over by sending us to the table of presence in the holy place where the written word comes alive by his spirit. I recall a time when this happened to me. I was reading God's word in the New Testament and I heard the voice of the Lord say to me, go to Psalm 91. When I heard this I obeyed but in my mind I said to myself "I already know Psalm 91."

Over the years I struggled with a fear of sickness and disease. I would quote scriptures from Psalm 91 and other healing texts to direct my mind and my thoughts. When I read Psalm 91 as the spirit of God instructed me, I felt as if I had never read this Psalm before. It was like God himself was talking directly to me saying, Karen, you dwell in the secret place of me, therefore these things you are fearing will never come near your dwelling. At that moment every fear I had instantly left me! I wept with joy for several days. I knew the written word of Psalm 91 but on that day God brought it to life in me by his spirit. I was forever changed. This does not mean that Satan still does not try to drop lies in my mind, but because of the revelation of God's word I laugh at the enemy and rebuke him.

The golden lampstand provides the light to the holy place representing illumination. The light could never go out. The priests had to make sure that there was always oil in the lamps. Jesus is forever the light of the world. His light will never go out. As the word of God becomes alive in us it will illuminate and renew our mind. *Ephesians 4:23 And be renewed in the spirit of your mind.*

The last item in the holy place was the altar of incense. The altar of incense was located just outside the holy of holies separated by a veil. The altar of incense was made of wood overlaid with gold. God instructed the priests to burn incense both morning and night to represent the prayers of his people flowing up to him. Our prayers are known as intercession. The incense consisted of several different spices that produced a sweet smelling fragrance to God. Jesus is our ultimate intercessor. Jesus always intercedes for his disciples and believers. Even now as Jesus is sitting at the right hand of the Father he is interceding for us.

Why is intercession (represented by the incense) closest to the holy of holies? We know what we do for others touches God's heart. When we are praying for someone else, our prayers please God. We are the prayer life of Jesus. We can also intercede for our petitions. Why is this so precious to God? It shows God that we need him. Our prayers are a sweet aroma to him. When Israel sinned, God would come rescue them when they cried out to him in prayer. God wants to know that his children need him. This is why Satan does not want us to pray. Our prayers draw us close to the holy of holies where we will experience his powerful presence. As we offer up prayers to God we are going from the holy place to the holy of holies. Intercession is the way to worship.

As intercession is taking place, worship begins. This worship moves us into the most holy of holies. The holy of holies contained the ark of the covenant which was made of wood and overlaid with gold. Within the ark was a jar of manna, Aaron's rod that budded and the two stone tablets of the law. The jar of manna represented Christ our life sustainer. God sustained the children of Israel with daily manna while they were in the wilderness. Therefore God's word is our manna. We have to eat God's word daily to be sustained. God told Ezekiel to eat the roll, again representing God's word. As we consistently spend time in the presence of God and in his word he will be sustain us. He will sustain us through every aspect of our life's challenges, both good and bad. Aaron's budded rod represents Christ the chosen high priest. There were jealous men and others who questioned Aaron's title of high priest, believing that they deserved the position more than him. Aaron being chosen as high priest represents Christ as the chosen High Priest. God told Moses to gather all the rods of each leader from each tribe, line them up and the rod that buds is his chosen one. Jesus Christ is the chosen one. The jealous men perished when the ground opened up and swallowed them.

The two stone tablets of the Ten Commandments was the law that the children of Israel were to keep. Spiritually it means that Christ kept the law by fulfilling it. Lastly, the lid that covered the ark was called the mercy seat. There were two angels on top facing each other looking down with their wings spread out. The angels looking down at the sprinkled blood represents when God looks at us he sees the blood of Jesus and not our sins. Everything in the holy of holies speaks directly to Jesus; therefore when you enter in we are going to meet Him intimately. When we begin to worship a breaking is taking place, a breaking away from our body and soul. *John 4:24 God is a spirit: and they that worship him must worship him in spirit and in truth.* In the holy of holies only spirit and truth can enter in. In the holy of holies you become one with Christ and Christ one with you. Jesus himself said in *John 14:20 At that day ye shall know that I am in my Father, and ye in me, and I in you.* In the presence of God we are coming together until we disappear and only see Christ. The ark of the covenant represents the presence of God and his presence dwelled in the most holiest place. God's presence cannot abide just anywhere, he will not abide where sin abides. He will not coexist with sin.

In God's presence everything about us disappears. It becomes all about Christ. This is where we can get caught up for hours. It is in God's presence that his glory is revealed. This experience of God's presence and his glory generally occurs in our personal time with him. When we are experiencing the manifestation of God's presence, we lose track of time. The world fades away. Our problems and cares of life are far from us. There is an awesomeness that is occurring and we cannot just come out of worship like we come out of a dance. When we finally come out, people will know we have been with God. Worship takes us to another level in Christ.

As a minister of the gospel the worship experience has to be a daily part of our life. As we enter into our private time with God, we start with praise and thanksgiving. We begin to thank God for the sacrifice of Jesus Christ on the cross and confessing our sins. Next, we allow God's word to cleanse us so that our life mirrors the life of Christ. As the word is cleansing us, the word begins to come alive in us. We weep and cry in our worship. The word supernaturally transforms our hearts. The word moves from a written format (words on the page of a Bible) to the illumination our mind. Next we begin to flow over into intercession pouring our prayers for others and ourselves. As we are praying, our flesh is dying and our soul (mind, will, emotions) is taking a back seat. Our spirit and the spirit of Christ begins to join together until all we see is Christ. In worship there is no praising or dancing or loud noises happening. Praise stirs up our soul. Worship stills our soul. Praise excites our emotions but worship quiets our emotions.

We desire to walk continually in God's presence. We desire to carry his anointing and glory in our life. This lifestyle takes spending significant time in worship. Worship is not a song. It's the intimate experience we have with God. The songs of worship are the result of being in the most holiest place with Christ. Songs of worship emerge from this experience. Many believe that it does not take all that. They will offer up a quick prayer and believe it will get the job done. If an answer to prayer is needed quickly, God will hear and will answer. If we want to walk close to Christ, a relationship has to be passionately kindled and developed over time. This sacrifice of time separates the boys from the men, the milk drinkers from the meat eaters, and the strong from the weak.

Our tabernacle diagram provides the measurements for the courtyard, the holy place and the most holy of holies. The courtyard measures 50x100x5 cubits, the holy place 10x20x10 cubits and the most holy of holies 10x10x10 cubits. The courtyard is the largest area where there is a lot of noise of dancing, thanksgiving and praise going forth. The courtyard is where the crowd is. It does not take a lot of time or effort to praise God. Christians who have accepted Jesus Christ are thankful for his sacrifice. Yet the majority has not gone any further in their relationship with him. They prefer to remain in the courtyard.

The holy place is much smaller and only a few make it in. Reading the word of God cleanses us and allows the spirit to bring the word to life in our soul. Many people do not read their Bibles. The word cannot come alive in us if we do not read it. Pastors all over the globe are trying to get their members to read and study the word of God because it is literally life giving. *Psalm 119:25 I lie in the dust; revive me by your word* (NLT). In the holy place we do not hear the noise of praise, but weeping and crying because of the revelation of God's word.

The holy of holies is the smallest area of the tabernacle and is just big enough for one person. Note that only one person, the high priest, was allowed in. We experience silence in the holy of holies, because God is revealing himself to us. We worship and experiencing his presence and glory. It is a personal manifestation. I have been in this place many of times. I was so caught up in the presence of God until no words would come from my mouth, I literally could not speak even if I tried. In the holy of holies, the glory of God brings supernatural light and illumination. There is no other light but God. When we are in the holy of holies, God shines on us so we can shine on others.

When we spend intimate time with God we work hard to reduce and eliminate distractions. A spiritual habitation has to be created similar to the spirit of God resting in the ark of the covenant located in the holy of holies. Purposely plan a time and place to meet God. When I know I am going to spend time with the Lord, I close my door and lock it. I tell my children to not interrupt me or come in my room. I do not want anything to break that intimate moment with my Lord. We cannot have outside distractions. Turn off your television, cell phones, and computers. Let's do whatever we need to do to keep from allowing interferences to disrupt this time with God. The Bible states in *Matthew 6:6 But thou, when thou prayest, enter into thy closet, and when thou hast shut thy door, pray to thy Father which is in secret; and thy Father which seeth in secret shall reward thee openly.* This passage means to go in a private place, meet God, and shut the door from any outside forces.

As ministers who lead God's people, we have to plan time to allow him to minister to us so that we can minister to those who we have been called to reach. It is vital that we know the directions God wants us to take for his people. Just as we schedule time for meetings and events on our calendar, we can block out special time for God. In my experience and based on the word of God, the best time to spend with God is in the early morning while everybody and everything is still quiet. Jesus rose early to spend time with his Father, *Mark 1:35 And in the morning, rising up a great while before day, he went out, and departed into a solitary place, and there prayed.* David spoke of praying in the morning, *Psalm 5:3 My voice shalt thou hear in the morning, O Lord; in the morning will I direct my prayer unto thee, and will look up.* Jesus spent many hours in prayer with his Father. If Jesus had to go to his secret place being the savior of the world, how much more do we need to do the same? We want God to show us his glory and give us his anointing and power. We want quick money and wealth, but we do not want to give God any time. If we are unable to do mornings, God knows all. We have to find dedicated time to spend privately with God. Once we start spending committed time with God, we will want to spend even more time with him. The more we practice being in the presence of God the smaller the things of world will become in our life.

Chapter 5

WOE EXPERIENCE

Isaiah 6:5

Then said I, Woe is me! For I am undone; because I am a man

of unclean lips, and I dwell in the midst of a people of unclean lips...

After Isaiah saw God's glory in this supernatural encounter, he learned more about himself. When we experience the presence of God, we not only see his glory, we experience his majesty. Most importantly we are exposed to who we are. The light of God's glory opened Isaiah's eyes to his own imperfections. At that moment, Isaiah realized very quickly that he was undone, unworthy and a sinner. He was amazed at God's great mercy which allowed him to see God's greatness despite his imperfections.

Sometimes God will get our attention and change us instantly. This is the case with Saul, who later was renamed Paul. He was on a mission to destroy every Christian. It is my belief that witnessing to Saul would not have convicted him or led him to say the sinner's prayer and accept Jesus as Lord. He needed an instant, supernatural change. Saul's instant conversion met him on Damascus road where he was blinded by the presence of God.

How can this be? Those who voluntarily go after God have already received Christ as their savior. Paul was not saved, he did not know Christ and probably would have never known him if the power of God had not knocked him off his feet. There are some people that God will go after himself. Isaiah knew he fell short of God's glory. Isaiah had a woe experience with great sorrow, distress, heart brokenness, despair, and depression. He understood that he needed deliverance. To be delivered successfully of any strongholds, habits or sins, first, we have to recognize and admit we have fallen short. Isaiah admitted what his problem was. *Isaiah 6:5 Then said I, Woe is me! For I am undone; because I am a man of unclean lips and I dwell in the midst of a people of unclean lips.* Isaiah did not look for excuses or reasoning to explain why he was this way. Let's admit our sins and not make excuses for them. If we desire to be God's ambassadors, our desire will be to live a holy and righteous life.

What woe experience have you had? We may not have seen what Isaiah saw but we can have a testimony that God revealed to us what we know was God alone.

A woe experience from God is not to be confused with a "woe is me" mentality. The "woe is me" mentality is demonstrated when we walk with our head hung low and feel sorry for ourselves. We walk around with a victimized spirit seeking attention from others. The difference is those who carry the "woe is me" mentality generally don't change their lives. They can stay in this state for a long period of time. Those who have a woe experience from God change instantly and remain changed. Our woe experience with God will cause us to repent and seek God's salvation, redemption and sanctification. One of our greatest examples is David. After Prophet Nathan revealed his sin, David had a woe experience. His eyes were opened and he responded. *Psalm 51:1-4 Have mercy upon me, O God, according to thy lovingkindness: according unto the multitude of thy tender mercies blot out my transgressions. Wash me thoroughly from mine iniquity, and cleanse me from my sin. For I acknowledge my transgressions: and my sin is ever before me. Against thee, thee only, have I sinned, and done this evil in thy sight: that thou mightest be justified speakest, and be clear when thou judgest.*

Both Isaiah and David recognized their woes and fell before the Lord asking for mercy. Throughout the Old Testament God said in many places "woe unto you," meaning destruction was coming because evil works were committed. *Isaiah 33:1 Woe to thee that spoilest, and thou wast not spoiled: and dealest treacherously, and they dealt not treacherously with thee.* God was speaking to the Assyrians who had destroyed others. It is far better to for us to recognize our own sins and have a woe experience than for God to say woe unto you. When God declared woe to nations and people, the outcome was frightening. As leaders and pastors it is important to stay in a repentant state. When God called woe to a person, it was because they would not turn from their wicked ways and because they did not heed to His warnings. The Lord let us know in *1 John 1:9 If we confess our sins, he is faithful and just to forgive us our sins, and to cleanse us from all unrighteousness.* God is loving and forgiving and he has endless mercies and grace. Why do many leaders still fall from their calling and lose sight of God? The benefit of having a woe experience is it reminds us that we cannot keep ourselves. We require the strength of God to walk upright. *John 15:5 I am the vine, ye are the branches: He that abideth in me, and I in him, the same bringeth forth much fruit: for without me ye can do nothing.* Even Jesus, while on earth said he could do nothing of his own, *John 5:30 I can do nothing on my own, I judge as God tells me. Therefore, my judgment is just, because I carry out the will of the one who sent me, not my own will* (NLT). Leaders and pastors that fall from their calling stop carrying out the will of the Lord. They prefer their own will and selfish desires.

It's no mistake; we will all make mistakes while fulfilling God's call in our life. Those who prosper in God give heed to the voice of God through revelation, the word, or through another person. King David was King when he fell into sin against Bathsheba and against her husband, Uriah. God spoke to David through his prophet Nathan. David repented and was godly sorrowful. David was changed forever and became a man after God's heart. The problem with many leaders today is that we do not want to listen when God brings correction to us through another man or woman of God. We feel intimated and often believe that the person is jealous or trying to tell us what to do. I have experienced this before where God put it on my heart to correct a young person in ministry. This person did not agree with the correction and continued to walk contrary to God's commandments. We are living in a time and generation where worldly intellect has increased and the knowledge of God has decreased. *2 Timothy 3:7 Ever learning, and never able to come to the knowledge of the truth.*

There is a benefit in having a woe experience. We have heard it said, "I had to go through that because it made me who I am today." *Psalm 119:1-2 It was good for me that I have been afflicted: that I might learn thy statutes. The law of thy mouth is better unto me than thousands of gold and silver.* Many would have never sought after God if we never had a woe experience. The life of suffering, pain and temptations causes us to seek God.

When we seek Him we will find him. When we find him and experience him, our life will never be the same. God let us know in *James 1:1-2 My brethren, count it all joy when ye fall into divers temptations: Knowing this, that the trying of your faith worketh patience.* God will allow us to go through various things in life to make us over for his glory. I had a woe experience that caused me to seek God like never before. The lesson I took away from that experience was to never trust my flesh. Though God may have delivered us in a certain area of our life, the devil will always come knocking at our door at some point of our life. Never think that we are strong enough not to fall into temptation. We are not strong enough to maintain ourselves by our own strength. Not only did I seek God intensely, but I gained wisdom and knowledge to help someone else.

Every experience will bring us closer to God if we allow it. God uses our experiences to strengthen our faith in him. God also uses these situations to increase our knowledge in Christ. Life's hiccups whether we enjoy them or not, helps us as a leader to teach and preach from the heart. Our life's lessons will prepare us. Experience is a powerful teacher. However, we must use caution and wisdom when giving personal experiences. Although God strengthens us and teaches us with powerful lessons with each experience we go through, we are not to enjoy falling to sin. Paul explained this same concept in *Romans 6:1-2 What shall we say then? Shall we continue in sin, that grace may abound? God forbid. How shall we, that are dead to sin, live any longer therein?* Therefore we are not to plan to sin to get closer to God or to gain more grace. *Galatians 6:7 Be not deceived; God is not mocked: for whatsoever a man soweth, that shall he also reap.* Although David repented from his sins and wrote the Psalm 51, he still suffered the consequences of his sins. The child that was conceived from David's illicit affair with Bathsheba died soon after birth. David also suffered great things from the lives of his sons.

Psalm 38 details David's mental anguish and physical pains he suffered as a result of his sin and disconnection from God. *Psalm 38:4-7 For mine iniquities are gone over mine head:*

as an heavy burden they are too heavy for me. My wounds stink and are corrupt because of my foolishness. I am troubled; I am bowed down greatly; I go mourning all the day long. For my loins are filled with a loathsome disease: and there is no soundness in my flesh. Once we have accepted Jesus Christ as our Savior, our desire is to not sin. If we do sin, we can go to Christ for forgiveness and grow from that experience as David did.

Our experience can possibly turn into a ministry, a teaching, or a book. We have heard the phrase "your misery is your ministry." Many people have become public speakers as a result of life experiences. Many cancer advocates have personally experienced the disease. I personally know someone who wrote a book after her experience with breast cancer. Many other books were written for similar reasons. We have books that teach us how to overcome divorce, depression, and having children on drugs. We desire to help someone else overcome or not experience the same thing we have experienced. Pastors and leaders can teach and empower our members to remain faithful to Christ.

Jesus Christ never sinned. Yet his experiences have taught us how to live in today's world. We live by Christ's experience. He taught us how to love by the way he loved. He taught us how to give by the way he gave. He taught us how to forgive by the way he forgave. Likewise, our life experiences teach others whether good or bad. Children that grow up in a home of alcohol and drugs are being taught the same behavior from their parent's experiences. We are teaching whether we think we are or not. If we have any influence on anyone they will learn things from our lives. Have you ever heard a child learning how to talk and begin to repeat aloud every word that is spoken around them? This is even more important if people look to us as their leader and trust in us. They will model our lives. Trending in our churches today is the common statement made from many of our leaders is "we are human and will make mistakes." Although this statement is true, it is being used to make excuses for not living as Christ has taught. Everything that comes from the head flows to the body. If the leader accepts these excuses the members will too. So then, the congregation will make the same statement, "I'm only human, God understands and know my heart." If the life of Christ is a blueprint for us to live by, people will use our life as a blueprint for their life. Paul stated to the Corinthians to use his life as an example to live by. *1 Corinthians 11:1 Be ye followers of me, even as I also am of Christ.* Our life will be followed as an example if we follow Christ or not, especially for those new in Christ.

We have to know our calling and take it very seriously because we may cause blessings or bleeding in a person's life. Paul teaches us to obey those that are over you. *Hebrews 13:17 Obey them that have rule over you, and submit yourselves: for they watch for your souls.* This is a prime example why leaders and pastors have to obey God and be led by the spirit of Christ. We watch over the souls of those we are called to lead and guide. According to this scripture your congregation is to obey you. We hear leaders quote 1 Samuel 15:22, obedience is better than sacrifice. Many state this scripture for the followers to obey what they are saying. Samuel clearly says to obey the voice of the Lord. If we are going to use this scripture, we have to be sure we are hearing and obeying God ourselves. If a person is not strong in the Lord, they will obey our words and our actions even if we are not following God. Therefore our words and actions are to edify and build the body of Christ and not tear it down.

Another trend that is being heard often from ministers and leaders is "let's be transparent." Transparency is good...up to a certain point. There is a thin line in trying to help others from falling into the same sin we fell into by being too transparent. It all depends on how we deliver our experience. For example, if we are explaining to our followers how we fell into alcohol abuse, we have to say more than God is a forgiving God and he will dust us off and sober us. We may take that message and feel as we can get drunk as long as we repent. We have to be able to tell the ugly side of being addicted to alcohol, for example, losing our job, losing our family or becoming homeless, etc. I was on the train one day on my way home from work. I overhead one man talking to another young man about becoming a pastor. The other young man said "how are you a preacher and you smoking…." at that point he lowered his voice. The young pastor responded, "man don't be telling people I do that, we all sin because we are human as long as you repent you are ok." This type of teaching from any leader will cause people to stumble and fall. Repentance is more than just being sorry, it means to turn away from sin. Once we repent and then go back into sin, we are not turning away from our sin. This is why I believe many leaders have lost great respect over the years. They are hiding who they truly are by looking for validation to remain the way they are. If we are struggling with a sin, seek God first in prayer. In his presence allow him to cleanse us as he did Isaiah. God is a deliverer. We can go to someone we trust, who is strong in their faith, to mentor us out of the sinful situation. I would not advise to unload our sins on our followers. This confession can be very damaging to members. Furthermore, Paul never told Timothy to be transparent he told him to preach sound doctrine. *2 Timothy 1:13 Hold fast the form of sound words, which thou hast heard of me, in faith and love which is in Christ Jesus.* When Isaiah accepted the call to go and give a message, he was not transparent in revealing that his mouth was unclean and he hung around the wrong people. He allowed God to clean him up first, then he went to preach the message God gave him to deliver. Stay on task with the message of Christ. If we are called to preach the gospel, preach the gospel. If you strongly feel like you need to be transparent and give your testimony make sure it's coming from God. Pray that the timing is right or we could possibly be revealing it to the wrong audience.

Many leaders have fallen to certain sins. Without having a woe experience we enjoy and want to continue in our sin. It is very dangerous not to have any convictions for our actions or ignore the convictions from the Holy Ghost. Not having convictions will cause us to continue and try to maintain our leadership position. We may succeed for a season but eventually the light will be shined on us. What is done in darkness will at some point always come to light. *Luke 8:17 For nothing is secret, that shall not be made manifest: neither anything hid, that shall not be known and come abroad.* Why is this happening? Many leaders and pastors are re-evaluating the word of God and changing the truth to a lie. They are accepting lifestyles and ways of living that are contrary to God's word. Without a woe experience a pastor can have a wife and a mistress for years. Without conviction, without fear and reverence for God, leaders can maintain a secret life for many years. The secret life will come to light. God never said how it would come out. Satan uses this very scripture to expose leaders to the public eye and media. How many times have you seen on prime-time news about pastors and leaders being exposed for their sins? This exposure may lead people to not desire Christ. As we begin to minister, let us begin to pray and ask the Lord to convict our heart of anything knowingly or unknowingly that is contrary to his word. We do not want to find ourselves as a leader with a seared conscious. *1Timothy 4:1-2 Now the spirit speaketh expressly, that in the latter times some shall depart from the faith, giving heed to seducing spirits, and doctrines of devils; speaking lies in hypocrisy: having their conscience seared with a hot iron.* In my everyday prayer I always pray that God would show me my error and faults and cleanse me from any unrighteousness.

Every leader needs someone to share accountability. This person must be able to tell you the truth. Friends may be too close to monitor our performance. I remember a time when my spiritual mother told me a hard truth about myself. Initially I felt some type of way but thank God I went home and thought about what she said to me. I had to admit to myself that she was correct in her saying. I thanked her for telling me the truth because it kept me from making a big mistake. As a leader we need a mentor, spiritual leader, or somebody who can tell us the truth. Hearing the truth does not always feel good and is not always accepted. I have learned over the years when we tell the truth about something people may think we are harsh or mean, although we say it in as much love as possible. If the truth condemns a sinful practice, some may not receive a message that rebukes them. Hearing the truth will make us free and prevent us from falling. *John 8:32 And ye shall know the truth, and the truth shall make you free.*

Once we have endured and made it through our woe experience we can now have a WOW experience. As we are strengthened in God, we will be able to preach and teach with power and demonstration because of our experience. God needs leaders to be his voice, his ambassador, and his example for those who do not know him. It is not meant for us to continue having woe experiences after woe experiences. We do not see in scripture where Isaiah experiences more than one woe experience. We do not see in scripture multiple Damascus road experiences for Paul. One time changed his life and he became a powerful apostle, who by inspiration of the Holy Ghost, wrote two thirds of the New Testament. Let's allow our woe experience to be transformed into a wow experience. It will cause us to soar in the plans God has for our ministry, reaching higher heights and deeper depths.

Teach like never before. Preach like never before. Move mountains by the spoken word. Lay hands on the sick so that they recover. Put demonic spirits to flight. Walk in your calling and experience a WOW.

Chapter 6

A PURGE CLEANSING

Isaiah 6:6-7

Then flew one of the seraphim's unto me, having a live coal in his hand, which he had taken with the tongs from the altar: And he laid it upon my mouth, and said, Lo this hath touched thy lips; and thine iniquity is taken away, and thy sin purged.

After a believer comes to the knowledge of Jesus Christ and accepts salvation by faith, there is a cleansing that takes place at that moment. Once we have accepted Christ, our spirit man is cleansed immediately. *1 John 1:9 If we confess our sins, he is faithful and just to forgive us our sins, and to cleanse us from all unrighteousness.* Throughout the Bible, numerous scriptures refer to washing, cleansing, pruning and purging. This is significant because from our mother's womb we were all born and shaped in sin. *Psalm 51:5 Behold I was brought forth in iniquity and in sin did my mother conceive me.* Sin cannot enter into heaven. To purge means to rid of any unwanted feeling, memory or condition. In our case, this refers to our sin. Synonyms for purge are, cleanse, clear, purify, wash, and absolve. After Isaiah's woe experience, the angel of the Lord came to him and laid a live coal upon his mouth and said, "...and thy sin purged." Those who have a woe experience from God, seek forgiveness, cleansing and restoration. This is what Isaiah was seeking.

A person with a "woe is me mentality" is not necessarily seeking change but rather sympathy. When David had a woe experience he called out to the Lord for forgiveness. David said in *Psalm 51:2 wash me thoroughly from mine iniquity and cleanse me from my sin.* Every believer is to be spiritually cleansed from all unrighteousness. We wash with soap and water daily to cleanse ourselves from earthly dirt stain. It is even more important to be cleansed spiritually. In our daily prayers we are to ask God to cleanse us from any unrighteousness. If we are physically dirty and never wash our body, we will begin to show visible signs of being dirty. Operating in sin and not being purged daily will show up in our life and ministry.

Baptism is an outward demonstration of what God has already done within when we are cleansed from our sins. We are emerged in water to bury our sins. We come up clean as a new person. Each of us who accepts Jesus Christ as our savior will go through a cleansing or purging. Baptism is generally done once. Yet we all need a spiritually refreshing from time to time. We need to allow God to renew our minds and our spirits. Peter explains how water, which was once used to destroy the human race, except for Noah's family, now, saves us by cleansing our mind. *1 Peter 3:21 And that water is a picture of baptism, which now saves you, not by removing dirt from your body, but as a response to God from a clean conscience.* As we go through life and minister, we may fall to sin. However, God will cleanse us each time when we go to him and confess our sins. Remember, the wages of sin is death (Romans 6:23). Let us make sure we go to God to purge any sin that may keep us from being cleansed. God told Jeremiah that he will cleanse his people. *Jeremiah 33:8 I will cleanse them from all their iniquity by which they have sinned against me, and I will pardon all their iniquities by which they have sinned against me and by which they have transgressed against me.*

As leaders it is vitally important that we allow God to purge or cleanse us from sin. To operate in the ministry of God while engaging in sinful activity is very dangerous. We are not to come before God dirty. God told Moses before he approached the burning bush to remove his shoes for he was standing on holy ground (Exodus 3:5). If God does not want dirty shoes near him, how much more does he not want a dirty life before him? God did not even want dirty clothes around him. *Exodus 19:10 And the Lord said unto Moses, go unto the people and sanctify them today and tomorrow, and let them wash their clothes.* God told Moses that the animal sacrifices could not have any illnesses, deformities or any defects. The choice animal had to be clean without any blemishes. *Deuteronomy 15:21 And if there be any blemish, or have any ill blemish, thou shalt not sacrifice it unto the Lord thy God.* Jesus walked the earth and healed all manner of sickness and disease to show his power and majesty. I also believe he healed them because he was holy and sickness could not hang around him or be in his presence. God has not changed. *2 Chronicles 7:14 If my people which are called by my name, shall humble themselves and pray, and seek my face, and turn from their wicked ways, then will I hear from heaven and will forgive their sin, and will heal their land.* God is always ready to heal us and cleanse us but he is waiting for us to seek his face. This is exactly what David did, he sought God concerning his sin against Bathsheba and in return God purged him.

Cleaning is a part of life. We clean our homes, our offices and our cars. Most people do not like to live in filth or dirt. Well the Holy Spirit does not like a dirty temple either. *2 Corinthians 6:16 And what agreement hath the temple of God with idols (sin)? For ye are the temple of the living God; as God hath said, I will dwell in them, and walk in them, and I will be their God, and they shall be my people.* Leaders, there is a standard of living that we are to live by in order to lead God's people. I have heard leaders get upset because they feel they cannot make a mistake or fall short without being criticized. Yes, we all fall short of God's glory. Leaders are held to a higher standard and are to set the example. Children need their parents to show them the way and be an example on how they should live. Although parents are not perfect, we still expected to live model lives before our children. Parents are leaders to their children. How many times have you heard a person blame the struggles in life on their childhood? When we visit a psychiatrist, the first thing they ask us is about our childhood. The parent is held accountable for the child's upbringing. If the world system will punish a parent for child endangerment or child neglect, then we know that God is not pleased as well. Likewise the sheep look to the shepherd for guidance. Shepherds can lead their sheep or flock astray if the life they live does not line up with the word of God. As much as leaders and pastors encourage their followers to read the word of God for themselves, many members will not study their Bibles. We look for our pastors to teach us and encourage us by showing the way. If we leaders stay before God in all things, he will keep us pure and clean. When we go before the sheep they will truly see God in us.

Once or twice a year we deep clean our home. When I was young, my mother would have all of us cleaning windows, walls, baseboards and so much more. When we deep clean, we go into cracks and crevices where we normally would not go. At the beginning of each year I purposely reflect on my life, my ways, personality and my actions. I am searching deep within myself for anything that may be in me that should not be. I also ask God to do some deep cleaning in me by searching my heart, *Psalm 139:23 Search me, O God, and know my heart: try me, and know my thoughts. Psalm 26:2 Examine me, O Lord, and prove me; try my reins and my heart.* Every pastor and every leader should allow themselves to be deep cleansed, in particular because of the nature of what you do for the Lord. Satan will always try to bring temptations, pride, and other ungodly things into our life.

Purging is not a pleasant feeling or experience. Chastisement is a part of purging and cleansing. Parents purge their children through correction. It may not feel good to the child but when he or she gets older they will be grateful for the cleansing. *Hebrews 12:6 for whom the Lord loveth he chasteneth, and scourgeth every son whom he receiveth.* This chastening by God is a form of cleansing to get us to a place in him, so that he may use us mightily for his glory.

David states in *Psalm 51:10 Create in me a clean heart, O God and renew a right spirit within me.* I believe we can ask God to cleanse and purge us daily. Temptations are prevalent in today's world. If we stay in prayer consistently we will find that these ungodly ways will not be common in our life. Part of the Lord's prayer says *...lead me not into temptation.* God's word is true. Temptations will not be a struggle as long as we maintain a relationship with him.

After we are purged, pruned and cleansed from our sins and unrighteousness, consecration is the next step. Consecration works with purging and cleansing. Consecration separates us from things that are unclean which have kept us bound. Consecration also means to walk in sanctification, holiness and purity. Have you ever noticed when we pray to ask God for forgiveness, at the same time we let him know how we will change and live better? We consecrate ourselves by deciding to live a holy life. David let God know what he would do if He forgave him of his sins. *Psalm 51:12-13 Restore unto me the joy of thy salvation and uphold me with thy free spirit. Then will I teach transgressors thy ways and sinners shall be converted unto thee.* David is consecrating his life and will begin to teach others. When God cleanses us and changes us, we are propelled to be consecrated, dedicated, and have a closer walk with him. To be consecrated does not mean we go to a special service, wear white and perform religious ceremonial acts. We can consecrated ourselves at home in our secret closet. Consecration changes our minds after we are clean to continue walking in the newness of life. Every year many churches have a ceremonial consecration service to start the New Year and dedicate their lives to God. I celebrate these leaders for hosting this kind of dedication service. I enjoy this service at my church. I want to encourage us to practice this self cleansing consistently throughout the year too. As long as we are in our mortal bodies, we will always need to be cleansed and purified.

God has called leaders to do a great work for him and he wants to do amazing things in us. God is not only looking for a willing vessel but he is also looking for vessels that are purged and consecrated. Joshua told the children of Israel to consecrate themselves. *Joshua 3:5 Joshua told the people, consecrate yourselves, for tomorrow the Lord will do amazing things among you.* If we want to do great and amazing things, we are to make sure we are living a cleansed and consecrated life. David also consecrated himself after he confessed his sins and after the child he conceived in sin died. *2 Samuel 12:20 Then David arose from the earth, and washed, and anointed himself and changed his apparel, and came into the house of the Lord, and worshipped.* Consecration follows our purging and cleansing process. We must first be purified. We repent and rid our lives of the daily dirt or the free radicals that live in our world. Then we consecrate our lives by changing, renewing and deciding not to get dirty again.

Praise and worship follows consecration. Praise is to give thanksgiving offerings or to applaud what someone has done. We give praise when our child has accomplished something or done a good work. We praise, applaud and offer thanksgiving to God for the work he has done in us. It is common courtesy to offer thanksgiving when a person does something for us. If someone pays our rent for the month, we are expected to give thanksgiving for this wonderful act. Praise is easy to do, it is not complicated. If someone does something for us we simply say thank you, which is praise. *Psalm 105:1 Oh give thanks (praise) to the Lord and proclaim his greatness; let the whole world know what he has done* (NLT). *Psalm 103:2 Let all that I am praise the Lord; may I never forget the good things he does for me* (NLT). In these two verses we see that praise is given to the Lord for the things he has done. How do you praise God? Praise can be rendered in several ways. We offer praise from our mouth. Praise him with the fruit of your lips (Hebrews 13:15) Praise expressions can also be given through dance. When the ark of the Lord was brought back to the city of David, David praised with gladness and danced before the Lord. *2 Samuel 6:14 and David danced before the Lord with all his might.* Praise can be given by clapping your hands. When God subdued enemies and nations, the children of Israel clapped their hands in praise. *Psalm 47:1 O clap your hands, all ye people; shout unto God with the voice of triumph.* All these expressions of praise are because of something the Lord did for his people. When God does something for us, we always stop and give him praise.

After David was cleansed of his sins he got up and consecrated himself through worship. Worship is defined as the feeling or expression of reverence and adoration for a deity. There is a major difference between praise and worship. Praise takes no effort, it is easy to say thank you. Worship is to love and adore someone for who they are and what they mean to you. For example, we can say thank you to a stranger for a kind act, but we typically do not love and adore the stranger because we do not know the person intimately. It is difficult to worship if we do not know Jesus Christ intimately. We can believe in him, believe that he was born in flesh, died on the cross, rose from the dead and ascended into heaven but not know him. In worship we spend private time with God. Worship will take us into the secret place of God which is an intimate place with him. When we get married, we take our spouse on a honeymoon. We go away with only our spouse to love and get to know each other. No one goes with us because it is an extremely private time for the newlyweds. Similar, worship is a private affair between us and Jesus. Worship is difficult to do if we have not built a relationship with God.

Leaders, worship is to be a way of life for us. God is looking for relationship with his people. God gives us directions and instructions to handle our everyday lives in our worship experience with him. Leaders and pastors hear from God in order to give followers what they need. Worship is to be an integral and daily part of a leader's life. In order to properly worship God, the Bible says in *John 4:23-24 But the hour is coming, and now is when the true worshippers shall worship the Father in spirit and truth, for the Father seeks such to worship him. God is a spirit and they that worship him must worship him in spirit and truth.* We worship God in spirit, but we can praise God and not be in the spirit. How is this possible you may ask? Everybody and everything that has breath can praise the Lord. *Psalm 150:6 Let everything that has breath praise the Lord.* However, as stated above in John 4:23 the Father seeks for those who will worship him. Why does God have to seek out true worshippers? In church we have pretenders and false worshippers. Praise and worship are very different. Our worship will be holy and sacred with our humility and reverence. If we stay in worship we will reduce the opportunities to fall into sin. The more we worship the closer we are to God and begin to learn his voice. We want to set aside quality time with him and not be rushed.

It's important to clear our minds and be quiet before we enter into the sacred place of God. Let our spirits become still and quiet so God may enter our hearts. I often play instrumental soaking worship music to help bring my mind to a point of focus and attentiveness. The room is filled with me and my Lord. I have been so deep in worship until I can not only feel his presence in the room, but I can also feel his presence on my physical body. I may feel heat or an electric sensation on my skin. I am weeping. I never want Him to leave. The more I share these moments with him, the more my problems and issues drift away from my thoughts. I never want to leave that place.

Once God cleanses us there is a feeling of freedom and freshness. Our ministry will reach heights and depths we have never known. God desires to bless his people with overflow. *John 10:10b I am come that they might have life, and that they might have it more abundantly.* This scripture not only state that we have life but have it more abundantly. More abundance means larger quantities! God was pleased with Solomon because he was more concerned about God's people than his own desires. God blessed Solomon with high levels of wisdom and accompanied with an abundance of wealth and riches. God wants to do the same for us. Remember the scripture *Psalm 84:11 For the Lord God is a sun and shield: the Lord will give grace and glory: no good thing will he withhold from them that walk uprightly.* Let's take the time to spend with our Father who is in heaven and we will live and be blessed according to the promises of God. Our ministries will prosper.

Chapter 7

KNOWING GOD'S VOICE

Isaiah 6:8

Also I heard the voice of the Lord, saying...

The million dollar question for many Christians is how to know God's voice. How do we distinguish God's voice from our own voice or from the voice of Satan? Many Christians struggle to understand if they heard God or their own thoughts. The Bible clearly states in *John 10:27 My sheep hear my voice, and I know them, and they follow me.* If Jesus says that my sheep hear my voice, why do so many Christians struggle to recognize his voice? Jesus said my sheep hear my voice and they follow me. We may hear the voice of God but not know it is him. It is hard to follow God if we are not sure he's talking to us. Samuel heard the voice of God calling his name. Samuel heard the voice of God and but Samuel thought it was Eli's voice calling his name. When God called me to evangelize, I clearly heard his voice but I thought it was my own thoughts. I heard his voice but I did not recognize it to be the voice of God. We must learn to hear his voice and know his voice.

God's voice can be heard in many different ways. God does not always speak to us the same way all the time. Jesus did not heal the same way. If we look to hear God's voice in only one way we will often miss his voice or not know he is speaking to us. In the dispensation of the old covenant God often used visions to speak to his priests and prophets. Isaiah heard God's voice while in a vision. This was common in the Old Testament. I believe God had to speak this way most often because the Holy Spirit did not dwell within man. Therefore God had to allow them to see things with their physical eyes and hear with their physical ears. The children of Israel did not hear or know the voice of God. During that time God only spoke his word to his priests and prophets, then they relayed the message to the people. Thankfully under the new covenant God is not only speaking to his leaders, but to any of us who will open our ear to hear.

I believe that there are three ways to hear and know God's voice. These are not exclusive; however, I believe they are the most common today. First, before we can hear God's voice, we must know that it is the Holy Spirit who dwells in us and reveals what God wants us to know. The Holy Spirit only speaks and gives us instructions as the Father instructs him. *John 16:13 Howbeit when he, the Spirit of truth, is come, he will guide you into all truth: for he shall not speak of himself; but whatsoever he shall hear, that shall he speak: and he will shew things to come.* If we have accepted Jesus Christ in our heart as your personal Savior, the Holy Spirit dwells in us.

There is a baptism of the Holy Spirit for service, power, witnessing and demonstration which occurred in Acts 2. Without the spirit of Christ we cannot survive or hear the voice of God. Therefore it is vital to know the Holy Spirit lives in us so we can hear God.

We hear the voice of God through his word. When we read the word of God, the Holy Spirit will take the written word and bring it to life in your spirit. *Hebrews 4:12 For the word of God is alive and powerful. It is sharper than the sharpest two-edged sword, cutting between soul and spirit, between joint and marrow. It exposes our innermost thoughts and desires (NLT).* Jesus states in *John 6:63 It is the spirit that quickeneth; the flesh profiteth nothing: the words that I speak unto you, they are spirit, and they are life.* God's word brings life and will change our life. No other book can do what the Holy Bible does. Other books may give inspiration, encouragement and knowledge but no other book can bring life.

We can read a passage in the Bible many times. Then on one particular occasion, the passage leaps off the page into our hearts. Something happens that's unique. The word comes alive in our spirit. Again as I mentioned earlier in this book, God lead me to Psalm 91. I read this Psalm many times before, but this particular time it was if I never read it. The Spirit brought the scripture to life in me and the things I feared instantly left. In order for God to reveal his word and bring it alive in us, we have to participant by actively and regularly reading his word. *Joshua 1:8 This book of the law shall not depart out of thy mouth; but thou shalt meditate therein day and night, that thou mayest observe to do according to all that is written therein: for then thou shalt make thy way prosperous, and then shalt have good success.* We do not know the day when God will give us a special revelation of his Word. We have to always be ready to receive from God. We can also hear God through the preached word. It does not matter if we are reading the word of God or if we hear the word of God through preaching. God's word is his word. When God's word goes out by preaching; the Bible says it will never come back to him void. *Isaiah 55:11 So shall my word be that goeth forth out of my mouth: it shall not return unto me void, but it shall accomplish that which I please, and it shall prosper in the thing whereto I sent it.*

The preaching of God's word is power to those who believe but foolish to those who perish. *I Corinthians 1:18 For the preaching of the cross is to them that perish foolishness; but unto us which are saved it is the power of God.*

We have heard our pastor preach the word of God and it appears as if he knew exactly what we were experiencing. God uses the preaching of the gospel to speak directly to us. We hear the voice of God through the Holy Spirit by reading and meditating on the word or through the preached word of our leader.

God used his written word to speak to me concerning my son. When I was away in college my son Stephen was only a toddler at that time. I worried constantly about what type of man he would become. I worried if he would end up on the streets of Chicago as a gang member, or find alcohol and drugs as a way of life. I did not want him to become a menace to society. One night I could not sleep, I tried everything to go to sleep until finally I got up went to my desk and opened my Bible. Literally all I did was open the Bible. I was not looking for any scripture in particular. When I opened the Bible and looked down, my eyes fell on Acts 6:8. Note that I spell my son's name the same way as Stephen in the Bible. *Acts 6:8 And Stephen full of faith and power.* That's all I saw and needed to see. Immediately I began to weep uncontrollably because I knew instantly without a doubt God was speaking to me concerning my son Stephen. I felt relieved that I did not have to worry any longer about what he would become as an adult. After that revelation of God's written word, I suddenly became very sleepy and was able to go straight to sleep. I am happy to testify that my Stephen is twenty eight years old, a husband and the father of three children. Stephen has never been in a gang, is not a drinker nor ever been on drugs. He is a born again Christian and loves God. God chooses whatever way he wants to speak to you.

Let's not box God into the way we want to hear him speak. If we do, we will miss God. We look for a word from God through certain pastors and prophets. If the person is not someone we know, we are reluctant to receive the message because he or she is not the prophet of our choice. The word that we really need may come from an unfamiliar source. Let's not limit God to specific leaders.

Another way of hearing God's voice is through our inner spirit or our heart. The world calls this the sixth sense. The voice of God through our inner spirit is to know something beyond intellect, understanding or explanation. It is sometimes an intuition, perception or premonition. This is the voice that is often missed or ignored. We have to be spiritually sensitive to not only hear his voice but also to know his voice. An intimate relationship with God is the key. The closer we get to God, the more sensitive we become in knowing his voice. Once we begin to recognize his voice we will know it. A few years ago, I was using a certain brand which I had used for many years. All of a sudden I began to sense that I needed to stop using it. I did not stop initially because I was not sure what I was feeling or hearing. Each time I used the brand, the sensing to stop using it increased more and more. One day as I was at the store to buy the product, without thinking, I purchased a different brand. I did not go back to my original brand. After I changed to the new product, I did not feel that way again. I felt a sense of peace. I realized and believe that God was speaking to me through my inner spirit.

How many times have we heard someone say they felt a premonition not to take a certain flight or to go a different direction than their usual way? Later they found out something tragic happened. If we feel very strongly in our spirit about something that we cannot explain, listen. It is through the inner spirit or inner part that God will speak and impart wisdom. *Psalm*

51:6 Behold you desire truth in the innermost being; And in the hidden part you will make me know wisdom.

God may also speak to us directly. It is more than having an inner sense of hearing but we actually hear the voice of God in our ear. This way of speaking to us may be a direct word. I have experienced this voice. The voice of God is not necessarily audible to others but audible in our ear. When God called me to ministry I was up late studying his word. It was very quiet in my house. I heard a voice say this exact word, "evangelize." When I heard it I looked around my house to see who said that. After seeing no one, I quickly dismissed what I heard and went back to reading God's word. Understand at that time I was unfamiliar with hearing God's voice in this way. As I began to continue reading, I heard the word "evangelize" for a second time. At that moment I began to fear because I did not know what was happening. When I heard God's voice it was literally like someone was speaking directly in my ear. It was audible inside my ear but not on the outside. I have heard God speak this way a few times but not often. When God speaks to me this way it's always a direct word. The last time God spoke to me in my inner ear is when he gave me direct instructions to launch the ministry he planned for me. Each time God spoke to me directly I was always in a quiet place. I strongly believe that it is important to spend quiet private time with God. It is often during those quiet moments that God speaks. If there is a lot of noise and distractions, we will most likely miss his voice. God often speaks in a still small voice. Elijah heard this still small voice of the Lord. Prior to God speaking in a still quiet voice to Elijah, he experienced strong winds, earthquakes and a fire. The prophet thought certainly God was in the boisterous weather. However, the Lord was not in those loud movements. He appeared in a still quiet voice.

When Elijah heard the voice he immediately got up. God's direct word will cause us to get up immediately. After I heard God tell me to start his ministry, I immediately began planning and executing his command. I never questioned what I heard because it was audible inside my ear and direct. We have to learn the voice of God. It will take time. Remember I said when

God called me to evangelize I did not know his voice. Years later when he spoke to me to start the ministry, I knew his voice. It took time and increasing my relationship with him to know his voice in that way. Why did Samuel not recognize God's voice when he called him those two times? The reason is he, as many of us today, did not recognize God's voice. *1 Samuel 3:7 Now Samuel did not yet know the Lord...* We have to know God in order to know his voice.

How do we distinguish between the voice of Satan and our own thoughts? Satan is a deceiver and is very cunning. Satan appeared to Eve very subtly. He was cunning. He deceived her. Eve clearly understood God's instructions not to eat of the tree of knowledge of good and evil. She believed that she and Adam would die if they ate. Eve was aware of this because she told the serpent this belief in Genesis 3:2-3. Satan was still able to trick Eve despite what she knew. The main way to know if God or Satan is speaking is to compare the thought being spoken to the word of God. It does not matter how intelligent or convincing it sounds, if it is opposite of what is in the word of God, consider it

Satan's voice. We see this ever so prevalent today in the world. Satan has deceived so many into believing that same sex relationship is the will of God, despite clear emphasis in his word that it is not. Satan will take what God hates and present it in such a way that it looks beautiful. Stick to God's word. If God is against it, do not allow Satan to gift wrap it and put a pretty bow on it and convince us that this is God's will.

To distinguish our own thoughts from God's voice is to know him. Our relationship with God will allow us to know the difference. Satan speaks through our thoughts and if we do not know God's word, we can be easily confused about who is speaking to us--God or our flesh. We have control over our thoughts and what enters our mind. We do not have to receive or accept thoughts that are contrary to the word of God.

I Corinthians 10:5 Casting down imaginations, and every high thing that exalteth itself against the knowledge of God, and bringing into captivity every thought to the obedience of Christ. We have the power to cast ungodly thoughts, wrong thoughts, lying thoughts and deceitful thoughts out of our mind. If we are not sure a thought is against the knowledge of God ask for the wisdom to know. To have wisdom is to have knowledge. *James 1:5 If any of you lack wisdom, let him ask of God, that giveth to all men liberally, and upbraideth not; and it shall be given him.* Without God's wisdom and discernment it is easy to fall to the voice of our thoughts or our flesh. Over the years I have learned the voice of God through studying the scriptures, through a praying relationship with God, and by mistakes. There have been times where I have mistaken my thoughts for God's voice. We will eventually find out whose words we are hearing, because God words will lead to increase. For we know God is not the author of confusion and would never lead us to a dead situation. Because of those mistakes I now know the difference. When I receive a word that I believe is from God, I ask myself two questions. Does it line up with God's Word? Do I have peace? If what we hear does not give us peace, we do not follow the voice. I recall a prominent pastor say if we do not have peace, don't do it, don't say it and don't go. When God speaks to us there will be a peace that follows. Remember when I said I felt a strong inner sense to stop using a certain brand. When I stopped using the product, I had great peace which confirmed that God was truly speaking to me. Sometimes we will not know unless we move out on what we hear. There are some areas that are not as clear as we would like for them to be. There are also decisions that we may hear in our minds that has nothing to do with sin or wrong living. For example we may be looking to start a new career or want a new job. There is nothing sinful about this and there is nothing in the Bible that says we cannot look for new opportunities. We do, however, want to go the path God has for us. Here's my example. I had been with the same corporation for many years doing the same thing. I began to desire a change. I started to pray and look for new opportunities with other companies. God had another plan for me. The desire I had in wanting to do something different was accurate. Wanting to change companies was not accurate.

I had an interview with one company but the position did not materialize. I filled out many applications and did not receive any calls. After going through this process for several months I began to think this was not God's will for me. I have been in the field for many years and with a master's degree, in my mind this should not have been a struggle. Little did I know that the exact position I was searching for was where I already worked. A few months later after giving up my search, I was promoted to the very position I desired at my existing company. Sometimes it takes moving out to know if it is God's will or not.

Every leader and pastor will need to know the voice of God because we receive instructions on how to lead his people. God spoke to Abraham to leave his country. Abraham heard him and obeyed his voice. God spoke to Moses and gave him instructions to lead the children of Israel. Moses obeyed. God spoke to his prophets Ezekiel, Jeremiah and Elijah and gave them instructions and messages to deliver to the children of Israel. The children of Israel depended on the priests and prophets to lead them, believing the messages came directly from God. The Bible says in *Romans 10:14 How then shall they call on Him in whom they have not believed? And how shall they believe in him of whom they have not heard? And how shall they hear without a preacher?* This scripture asks how anyone can know God without hearing the gospel through the preacher or leader. Therefore, we have to know and hear God's voice to preach and teach. If a leader does not know God's voice, how then can we lead or pastor others? Every believer has the capability to hear and know God's voice. Many Christians do not practice the spiritual disciplines to know the voice of God. They look to their leaders and pastors for guidance, instructions and encouragement. It is imperative for pastors and leaders to know the voice of God, to obey it and follow what he is saying. When we are hearing God's voice accurately, God's people receive comfort, hope, encouragement, peace, joy, and strength. We understand it is not the preacher that gives us these benefits, but it comes with our leader's obedience to the voice of God. I have received a word from my pastor either by the preached word or a direct prophecy from God which strengthened me. Why did this happen? I was strengthened because my pastor was sensitive to the voice of God and was obedient in delivering or speaking to me what God gave him. Some leaders have become consumed with their own fleshly desires that they have lost sight and focus of God. When we are answering the call of God on our life, it's important to remember that it's God's call, not our call.

Chapter 8

MOVING AT GOD'S VOICE

Isaiah 6:8

...Whom shall I send, and who will go for us? Then said I,

Here am I; send me.

When Isaiah heard God ask who will I send, he heard God's voice clearly before he answered the call. God prepared Isaiah for the assignment. Isaiah's relationship was made right with God. He was able to hear God's voice, know his voice and move at his voice. Our relationship with God helps us know the voice of the calling, the voice of preparation and the voice to move out. When we hear the voice to move, it is exciting to finally begin the work for which God called us. Despite the challenge of the assignment, we know that the Holy Spirit is with us. We experience a peace when we do his will. Sometimes God will call us to do or say something that is unpopular to the world and church. Isaiah answered God's call to deliver an unpopular word to the children of Israel, but he obeyed nonetheless. On the other hand if we do not move at the voice of God, it can hinder our assignment. When we decide not to move at the voice of God, we will miss opportunities, lack peace in our spirit, and possibly commit a sin of omission.

In chapter 2, I talked about missed doors or opportunities. When God is ready to save someone, he chooses us to be his witnesses. If we miss the opportunity to bring the person to Christ, it is a missed door. When we hear the voice of God tell us to do something we have to move. The individual that God wants to receive salvation will still receive it but through another person who will obey and move at the voice of God. I remember my pastor telling the congregation that God gave him instructions to use a visual demonstration to help explain a point that he was making. He decided not to give the demonstration and finished his sermon. After he finished speaking, the pastor of that particular church gave the same visual demonstration that God told my pastor to give. This is a prime example that God's plan will be carried out regardless if we move at his voice or not. God will always find someone he can use! One day God spoke to me through my inner spirit to go pray for a woman with a terminal illness. I knew I was supposed to pray for her but I was too afraid to move at his voice. After the woman died I felt awful and had no peace until I repented before the Lord. I committed a sin of omission because I knew I was supposed to pray for her. Sin of omission is when we neglect or fail to do something God had commanded us to do. *James 4:17 Therefore to him that knoweth to do good, and doeth it not, to him it is sin.* Jonah committed a sin of omission when he failed to obey and move at the voice of God to speak to the people of Nineveh. As a result of his omission and trying to go a different direction he was swallowed up by a great fish for three days and three nights. Jonah was given a second opportunity to obey the voice of God. We may not receive a second chance like Jonah. I did not have a second opportunity to pray for the woman because she died. It is best to move the first time we hear the voice of God.

When we hear God's voice to carry out an instruction, let's move quickly even if we do not understand the command. I travel on public transportation to and from work. I do not talk much during the ride. One day as I was sitting on the bus I looked up and saw a young man in his teens. God gave me a word for the young man. I was hesitant at first because I was not comfortable speaking in that way. I sat and sat as we were coming to the end of the line. The sense to talk to the young man grew stronger and stronger in my heart. I got off the bus and waited for him to get off. I told him what the spirit of the Lord gave me to say. The young man said thank you and walked away. I did not know how he felt about the message. I do not what the result was. I obeyed and moved at the voice of God. I believe that God wants to know if he can trust us to carry out his plan. Sometimes he will give us a small assignment to see if we will carry it out. He wants to see if he can give us greater responsibilities. *Matthew 25:21 His lord said unto him, well done thou good and faithful servant: thou hast been faithful over a few things I will make thee ruler over many things.* When we know God is calling us to perform an act, we have to move immediately. One day I was walking to the train station. I saw a man looking for food in the waste trash. I felt very strongly in my spirit to buy him some food. You may ask why did I need to hear God's voice to feed the poor when this is something Christians are to do. True, I give money to the homeless from time to time. This time was different and I felt it in my spirit. I took the man into a fast food restaurant and purchased food, drink and dessert for him. The man was very grateful and thanked me. I walk the same route to the train every day and I never saw that man before nor did I ever see him again. Sometimes I wonder if I entertained an angel unaware. *Hebrews 13:1-2 Let brotherly love continue. Be not forgetful to entertain strangers: for thereby some have entertained angels unawares.* Whether he was an angel or not I heard the voice of God and I moved.

Moving at the voice of God will take us into our destinies. Let's discuss the use of a navigational system to get to our destinations. Unless we move from a parked position to drive, we will not carry out the will of God for our life. I travelled to Whitewater, Wisconsin. I used my navigational system because I never been there before and was unfamiliar with the area. We have to know the voice of God and obey. He sends us into unknown and unfamiliar places. I had no clue as to where I was going. I kept hearing my navigational system give me instructions. I obeyed the voice and followed its instructions. The surroundings were new to me but I was not afraid. I trusted in my navigational system and I knew it would get me to my final destination. Just as we trust navigational systems, we are to trust the voice of God. Let's obey and go where he is sending us.

Genesis 12:1 Now *the Lord had said unto Abram, get thee out of thy country, and from thy kindred, and from thy father's house, unto a land that I will shew thee.* In this scripture God speaks to Abram and tells him to go. God does not tell Abram where he is going but says to him, "I will shew thee." Blind trust. Abram had to believe God. He had no idea where he was going. He heard the voice, obeyed and moved. When God was ready to deliver the children of Israel from Egypt he chose Moses. *Exodus 3:10 Come now therefore, I will send thee unto Pharaoh that thou mayest bring forth my people the children of Israel out of Egypt.* Notice God said, "come now." When God is ready for us to move, it is a "right now" assignment. Moses obeyed God's instructions. He first asked God a few questions. He did not understand how this would be possible. It is ok to ask God questions concerning the mission he has for us as long as we are asking from a pure heart not from fear and doubt. God knows the heart of every man. Remember when the angel of the Lord told Mary that she would conceive by the Holy Ghost. Mary asked how can this happen since she had never been with a man. Mary's questions were out of a pure heart and the angel answered her. On the other hand Zechariah, Elizabeth's husband questioned the angel about how could Elizabeth conceive when she had been barren for many years and he was old. Zechariah asked this question out of doubt and unbelief and not a sincere heart. Zechariah was struck dumb and could not speak until the child was born.

If we question God about what he has called us to do, let's make sure we are asking sincerely and not because we do not believe. God called Noah to build an ark for a great flood that would kill all of mankind except for Noah's family and the animals. Noah had to truly trust the voice of God and move at his instruction to build such a detailed magnificent boat. God gave Noah instructions to build the ark and Noah obeyed. Noah had to move immediately at the voice of God because his obedience was time sensitive. *Genesis 6:22 Thus did Noah; according to all that God commanded him, so did he.* When Jesus was choosing his twelve disciples he saw both Peter and Andrew by the Sea of Galilee. Jesus called them; *Matthew 4:19-20 And he saith unto them, follow me, and I will make you fishers of men. And they straightway left their nets, and followed him.* Peter and Andrew immediately moved at the voice of the savior.

Not only did the men of God in the Bible move at his voice but the elements hear, know and obey his voice. *Matthew 8:26 ...Then he (Jesus) arose, and rebuked the winds and the sea; and there was a great calm.* Jesus' disciples marveled and were astonished at how the winds and the sea obeyed him. Animals obeyed the voice of God. God called two of every kind of animal to come to Noah. The animals heard the call, obeyed the voice and went into the ark. If the wind, seas, and animals can hear the voice of God and obey why do humans struggle? God gave us intellect and understanding. We reason with what we hear and become doubtful or walk in unbelief. These things will cause us not to move at his voice. We are reminded by Jeremiah what can happen when we do not open to hear from God. *Jeremiah 17:23 But they obeyed not, neither inclined their ear, but made their neck stiff, that they might not hear, nor receive instruction.* When we purposely incline our ear to the Lord, we will know his voice and move at his voice. There are great benefits when we open our ear to hear and obey. *Isaiah 55:3 Come to me with your ears wide open. Listen, and you will find life. I will make an everlasting covenant with you. I will give you all the unfailing love I promised David (NLT).*

Think about when we were children. When our mother or father called us, there was no doubt who was calling us. We knew their voice. When they gave us instructions we obeyed. We have children and expect them to obey our voice. God expects us to obey him. Samuel made it clear that obeying God's voice is always better than observing religious ceremonies. *1 Samuel 15:22 And Samuel said, hath the Lord as great delight in burnt*

offerings and sacrifices, as in obeying the voice of the Lord?
Behold, to obey is better than sacrifice, and to hearken than the
fat of rams.

It is important when we hear the voice of God give us
instructions and that we do not stall or hesitate. Satan will use our
hesitation for his advantage. Satan will try to bring confusion to
our mind and cause us to doubt what we heard. Remember the
saying, "If you think too long you think wrong." If we stall too
long we will question what we heard and question if it was from
the Lord. Even if we do not always understand what God is
asking us to do, we have to be like Abram and obey. As we go,
God will show us the way. Remember how Eve allowed the
serpent to get in her head. If she had rebuked Satan immediately,
he would not have been able to convince her to go against what
she knew. When we know God is speaking to us about
completing an assignment for him we cannot say, "well let me
think about it." Thinking about the assignment becomes a conduit
and an open door for Satan to pour questions and doubt in our
mind. When I heard the voice of God give me instructions about

ministry, I immediately took action. I did not question it because I know my Father's voice. Satan had no chance to plant any negative thoughts in my mind. Even as I am walking out the instructions God gave me, Satan will try to tell me this task is too hard or I will not be able to accomplish it. I immediately rebuke him. Because I have learned the tricks of the enemy over the years, I recognize when he tries to show his head. Even if we accept the call for our life, Satan will always look for ways that will cause us to quit, give up and abandon our mission. He will do anything to try to destroy the church and leaders.

According to a research study by Pastoral Care Inc., 50 percent of pastors starting out will not last five years. More than 1,700 pastors left the ministry every month in 2016. The number one reason why pastors left the ministry was because church people were not willing to embrace the goals of the pastor. Pastors believed God wanted them to go in one direction, but the people were not willing to follow their lead. These are alarming statistics but not surprising. The leaders of the Bible faced similar problems but they stayed the course. As Moses followed God's direction, the children of Israel complained, murmured, made a golden idol to worship and wished to be back in Egypt. What kept Moses from throwing in the towel? The children of Israel did not listen to a word Jeremiah spoke to them. What kept him from giving up? Even Paul had some frustrations in his ministry. Paul had to rebuke the Galatians for quickly deserting what they were taught. *Galatians 1:6 I marvel that ye are so soon removed from him that called you into the grace of Christ unto another gospel.* Paul did not get to the point of abandoning the ministry. Our relationship with God is of the utmost importance if we are not to become a part of these unfortunate statistics. Every individual has to give an account for themselves. Let's move at voice of God despite what is going on around us. Obedience is critical even if our followers do not go with us. Although the children of Israel would not listen to Jeremiah, he was told to warn the people anyway. God helped Jeremiah by telling him not to look at their faces. Let's keep our focus on God's word and our eyes on him. There will be many people who will not make it to heaven because they did not listen to God's sent men and women.

Jesus taught a parable about a rich man who asked father Abraham to send Lazarus to warn his brothers not to come to the tormenting place. How did Abraham respond? *Luke 16: 29- 31 Abraham saith unto him, they have Moses and the prophets; let them hear. And he said, nay, father Abraham: but if one went unto them from the dead, they will repent. And he said unto him, if they hear not Moses and the prophets, neither will they be persuaded, though one rose from the dead.* There will be many who will not listen to the message of Christ. Many will rebel against the message of Christ. Some will turn away. Do not allow Satan to push you to abandon ship.

When we do not move at God's voice, it hinders our future assignments and to be given even greater assignments. I watched a YouTube teaching by Kenneth Hagin. He explained how God used him to pray for a woman on her deathbed and she was healed. The Lord let him know the reason he was able to give him the assignment of healing was because he obeyed God's voice to bless another preacher financially. Kenneth Hagin explained he was hesitant and did not want to give the preacher the amount God had told him because it would leave him with hardly any money left. Nevertheless he obeyed. If we never understand the reason why God is asking us to do something, let's move at his voice anyway. Most often we will not understand the instructions of God at that moment. Even when we go through trials and tribulations, we will not always know why. However, later at some point God will show us the reason. We will be glad we obeyed and went through the valley. God has a plan and an agenda for every believer. Don't try to figure it out, just obey and move. Our assignments often start small. As we obey God we know that he can trust us to carry out his will. He will assign to us greater works. Today we live in a fast age. Quick money. Quick blessings. Quick power. Quick platforms. Before we receive a college degree, we have to first pass each course. This process can take several years depending on the program. We have to prove ourselves by obeying our instructor, completing the assignments and passing the exams before we can go to the next class. We start with business 101, a beginner's course. When we pass the first course, we proceed to business

102. God operates in much the same way. Depending on our level of maturity, we can sometimes skip a class and go to the next level. If God is pleased with our obedience and dedication to him, he may move us further and faster in the next assignment. Our ability to grow in God, hear his voice and move at his voice is all dependent on us.

When Elisha asked for a double portion of Elijah's spirit, Elijah responded "you have asked a hard thing." Why was this request a hard thing? It was a hard thing because Elijah could not grant the request, only God could. Secondly, I believe it is a great responsibility to carry such an anointing. The fact that God granted Elisha the double portion lets us know that God trusted Elisha to carry out his will. We must hear the voice of God and move at his voice no matter what task is before us. Elisha's ministry is known as one of the most influential in the Bible. Elisha basically moved to the head of the class. Can God move you to the head of the class? It's important that we move whether we take one class at a time or become enrolled in an accelerated class. When we move we proceed, we progress, we advance, we stir and we shift. Our moving benefits us and those we are called to because we are obeying the voice of God.

Pastors and leaders, in order for us to go to the next place in our ministry or advance to the next season, we have to move. The only way we can move is to hear the voice of God and obey. There is no other way. There is no shortcut we can take. There is a song that says you can't go over, you can't go under, you can't go around, you must come in at the door. Our door is the door of obedience. When we are moving forward as God instructs, we are pressing forward toward the goal and prize. *Philippians 3:13-14 Brethren, I count not myself to have apprehended: but this one thing I do, forgetting those things which are behind, and reaching forth unto those things which are before, I press toward the mark for the prize of the high calling of God in Christ Jesus.*

Chapter 9

THE UNPOPULAR WORD

Isaiah 6:9

And he said, Go, and tell this people, Hear ye indeed, but understand not; and see ye indeed, but perceive not.

When God asked who shall we send and who will go for us, Isaiah immediately answered, here am I; send me. Isaiah did not know what the assignment was before he volunteered for the job. Isaiah's assignment was not a message that would cause his listeners to shout with praise or jump for joy. Isaiah was sent to preach to a people who would not listen and would not understand. As he preached their hearts became dull, their ears would be heavy and their eyes would shut. No preacher wants to preach to a congregation that does not receive the message of God. It is very difficult to preach to people and know that they are not receiving anything we say. This assignment was difficult for Isaiah because he asked God how long he must continue to preach this unpopular word. While the word itself is not unpopular, it becomes unpopular to those who do not want to hear or receive it. Any word that calls for correction, rebuke or reproof is not popular among those who are not willing to hear and receive. God answered Isaiah; *Isaiah 6:11-12 Then said I, Lord how long? And he answered, until the cities be wasted without inhabitant, and the houses without man, and the land be utterly desolate, and the Lord have removed men far away, and there be a great forsaking in the midst of the land.* Why was the message of Isaiah unpopular to the people? The children of Israel were comfortable in their sinful life. They rejected the word of God. Isaiah had to preach to them anyway. How would you feel if you knew God was sending you to a nation to preach God's good news but it would not be received? We would most likely say what's the use, why make the effort?

The word of God is probably more unpopular today than it has ever been in history of mankind. The Bible states in *1 Thessalonians 2:3 Let no man deceive you by any means: for that day shall not come, except there come a falling away first, and that man of sin be revealed, the son of perdition.* We are already seeing this evidence of falling away. Despite the fulfillment and revelation of God's word, leaders and pastors still have to preach the gospel of Christ even if no one receives it. It is critical to understand that if we believe God has called us to ministry and to preach the gospel, we will be faced with a generation of people who do not want to hear the word of God or endure sound doctrine. As Christ's return approaches men will be lovers of themselves. *2 Timothy 3:1-4 This know also, that in the last days perilous times shall come. For men shall be lovers of their own selves, covetous, boasters, proud, blasphemers, disobedient to parents, unthankful, unholy, without natural affection, trucebreakers, false accusers, incontinent, fierce, despisers of those that are good, traitors, heady, high minded, lovers of pleasures more than lovers of the God.* In the midst of this great falling away can we leaders still stand and preach the gospel? We may be criticized and be verbally attacked. The word of God is unpopular to the world and even to some Christians. They feel that God's word has no relevance today. However we know from

Hebrews 13:8 Jesus Christ the same yesterday, and today, and forever.

When Isaiah went to preach to the children of Israel they did not receive the message because they were enjoying their sinful lifestyle. To line up with God's word meant they would have to turn away from their wicked ways, put away their idols, and turn away from sexual immorality. Anytime we preach against the desires of the flesh, we will have opposition. When a leader comes against sin, the world will fight back. Today even Christians are attacking unpopular word. Churches do not want pastors and leaders to preach against sin. They desire to hear messages that make them feel good. Messages of wealth, health, and empowerment words are the only type of sermons they want to hear. Although these are areas that should be taught and preached, corrective messages are to be taught too. This is the unpopular word. Paul told Timothy to be strong in his preaching by the grace of God. *Timothy 2:3 Thou therefore endure hardness, as a good soldier of Jesus Christ.* Paul shares with Timothy that his suffering is because he preaches the good news of Jesus Christ. Paul also tells Timothy no matter the season, the gospel must be preached. *2 Timothy :4 Preach the word; be instant in season, out of season; reprove, rebuke, exhort with all long suffering and doctrine.* What is a leader to do when he or she faces hardship? What are you going to do? Will you walk away from ministry? Will you walk away from your assignment?

Paul teaches Timothy that in the midst of his suffering, continue to teach and stand on the word of God. Paul and Timothy had a father and son relationship. Poet Langston Hughes wrote a poem called "Mother to son" that is similar to what Paul was saying to Timothy.

Mother to Son

Well, son, I'll tell you:

Life for me ain't been no crystal stair.

It's had tacks in it,

And splinters,

And boards torn up,

And places with no carpet on the floor

Bare

But all the time

I'se been a-climbin' on,

And reachin' landin's,

And turnin' corners,

And sometimes goin' in the dark

Where there ain't been no light.

So boy, don't you turn back.

Don't you set down on the steps

'Cause you finds it's kinder hard.

Don't you fall now

For I'se still goin', honey,

I'se still climbin',

And life for me ain't been no crystal stair.

By: Langston Hughes

Looking back at the statistics mentioned in chapter 8, the question was asked, what is the number one reason why pastors are leaving the pulpit? The answer according to the survey said pastors feel they are going in the direction led by the Holy Ghost but the people do not want to follow. As you read throughout the

Old Testament you will find that the children of Israel were rebellious against many of God's chosen leaders. So we can see this is nothing new. The question then becomes what is the difference between the leaders of old and today's leaders? There are many answers to this questions that can be considered. Did we step into a role that we were not called to? Did we move forth prematurely? Did we understand the assignment? Are we trying to please man instead of God? No matter which answer we choose, the answer will always point to man. One thing for sure the answer does not lie with God. God equips and prepares those he calls and chooses. *Romans 8:30 Moreover whom he did predestinate, them he also called: and whom he called, them he also justified: and whom he justified, them he also glorified.* God will not start a work in you then set you up for failure. *Philippians 1:6 Being confident of this very thing, that he which hath begun a good work in you will perform it until the day of Jesus Christ.*

Due to these alarming statistics, it is easy to see how a Biblically compromised message is easily preached today. It's more inviting to preach feel good messages that will leave the congregation dancing and praising God. Perhaps we fear members may leave the church or not support the ministry financially. We must employ messages of restoration and promises as well as messages of correction, reproof and rebuke. In Revelations John was caught up in the Spirit on the isle of Patmos. Jesus showed him the seven churches of Asia. Jesus told John to write letters to the seven angels (pastors) of the seven churches. Jesus praised each church for their steadfastness in him. Yet he had a complaint against most of the churches. The purpose of these letters was to send correction and warning to the churches. Jesus had a complaint against the church of Thyatira for allowing Jezebel to teach and seduce the people through sexual sins. *Revelations 2:18-20 And unto the angel of the church in Thyatira write; these things saith the Son of God, who hath his eyes like unto a flame of fire, and his feet are like fine brass; I know thy works, and charity, and service, and faith, and thy patience, and thy works; and the last to be more than the first. Notwithstanding I have a few things against thee, because thou sufferest that woman Jezebel, which calleth herself a prophetess, to teach and to seduce my servants to commit fornication, and to eat things sacrificed unto idols.* Notice all of the Revelation letters greeted the angel of the church. God was talking directly to the leader or the pastor of the church to deliver a message to the congregation. Whatever the church is in need of God speaks through the leader and the leader is designed to deliver the word to the people. Even if the word is unpopular and difficult to deliver we have to obey or we will be held accountable. The church will suffer because of our disobedience. Secondly, we see that Jesus first acknowledged the good things about church. We can always acknowledge and give praise to our followers for the good things they do. Jesus then gives the complaint. It is the pastor's responsibility to correct the church and members as God leads. For both the church of Ephesus and Pergamos Jesus called for them to repent. Pastor and leaders, it is our responsibility to correct and call people to repentance. If they do not repent then it is no longer on our hands. As leaders we have to preach more than material gain and success. The Bible states, *Mark 8:36 For what shall it profit a man, if he shall gain the whole world, and lose his own soul?*

The Bible states we are in a time when people do not want sound doctrine. *2 Timothy 4:3 For a time is coming when people will no longer listen to sound and wholesome teachings. They will follow their own desires and will look for teachers who will tell them whatever their itching ears want to hear (NLT).* Let's not be that leader who does what the people want instead of what God wants. Aaron the priest allowed the children of Israel to convince him to make a golden calf for them to worship while Moses was on the mountain with God. *Exodus 32:1 When the people saw how long it was taking Moses to come back down the mountain, they gathered around Aaron. "Come on," they said, "Make us some gods who can lead us (NLT).* When Moses came down from the mountain he asked Aaron what have the people done to you to make you do such an evil sinful thing. Aaron then turned the blame back on the people. *Exodus 32:21-22 And Moses said unto Aaron, what did this people unto thee, that thou hast brought so great sin upon them? And Aaron said, let not the anger of my lord wax hot; thou knowest the people that they are set on mischief.* When God gives us instructions let's not allow the people to convince us to do something else. Preaching the unpopular word may not feel good, but it will allow the truth of God's word to set people free. When we do not share God's instructions, we are held accountable for the assignment because it was given to us.

As a mother I had to sit my children down and have an unpopular conversation with them. I knew before we began the discussion that they were not going to like what I had to say. It did not matter to me. I knew it would hurt for a moment but will benefit them later. I believed they would be thankful. When we receive a hard truth, it's difficult to swallow initially. After thinking about the feedback, we realize later we needed it. Thinking about our own lives, how many times have we looked back on our childhood and praised God that our parents chastised us as kids. We were not allowed to go and do whatever we wanted. This discipline made us better adults. During our childhood, we may have believed that our parents were too hard on us. As we grew older and wiser, we now know it was for our best! Having the unpopular conversation is not only for the church. Managers and business owners have to call employees into the office and have difficult conversations. If the manager fails to have these conversations, it can have a negative impact on the company.

Moses had spent 40 wonderful days in the mountain with God. As he began his descent to come back to the people, he witnessed utter chaos. Aaron was assigned to be the leader and he let the people tell him what to do. We leaders have to take our stand on God's word and not let man influence us to disobey him. A leader has to make tough decisions every day. We are responsible for having those unpopular conversations.

Ezekiel was given the task of delivering an unpopular word. God told Ezekiel that he had to eat the whole scroll despite the contents of the scroll. His assignment was to deliver the message. Whatever God puts before us leaders, we have to eat it and deliver the message. *Ezekiel 3:1 The voice said to me, "son of man, eat what I am giving you, eat this scroll! Then go and give its message to the people of Israel" (NLT).* Before Ezekiel ate the scroll he saw what was on it. *Ezekiel 2:10 And I saw that both sides were covered with funeral songs, words of sorrow and pronouncements of doom.* Not every message we preach or teach will be a happy joyful message. It will not always be received joyfully. Although Ezekiel had to deliver this unpopular word, God made sure it would not be unpleasant for him. God's unpopular message may be sour in the mouth of his people. As his servants, he will make the unpopular message taste like honey to us because of our obedience. *Ezekiel 3:3 "Fill your stomach with this," he said. And when I ate it, it tasted as sweet as honey in my mouth (NLT).* By filling his stomach with the message, Ezekiel would have to digest, retain and understand the message for the people. God will make us peaceful while we deliver a difficult word. Ezekiel is informed that his audience will not receive his message. *Ezekiel 3:7 But the people of Israel won't listen to you any more than they listen to me! For the whole lot of them are hard-hearted and stubborn (NLT).* He was still commanded to deliver the message. It is not up to the congregation to decide what they want to hear. We are not to fear what our members might think or say. Our assignment is to speak what God wants. God made Ezekiel as hard-hearted as the children of Israel. He was not permitted to get emotionally connected or walk in fear. He had to deliver the contents of the scroll he ate. *Ezekiel 3:8-9 But look, I have made you as obstinate and hard-hearted as they are. I have made your forehead as hard as the hardest rock! So don't be afraid of them or fear their angry looks, even though they are rebels (NLT).* In other words, God will strengthen us to deliver unpopular words.

Jesus gave messages of hope and messages of rebuke. In the gospels of Matthew, Mark, Luke and John, we see that Jesus had to give harsh teachings and words. Jesus turned over the tables of moneychangers from the temple. He reminded the people that God's house is a house a prayer (Matthew 21:21). Jesus corrected his disciples. Jesus told Peter if he did not allow him to wash his feet he would not belong to him (John 13:8). Jesus also rebuked Peter for saying his death would not happen (Matthew 16:23). Still the disciples struggled to believe despite the parables and miracle demonstrations. Jesus fed five thousand people from a seed of two fish and five loaves of bread. Despite these supernatural provisions, they were amazed and could not understand who Jesus was. He calmed the sea. He rebuked the tormenting spirit from a young boy. Jesus replied with a true word and strong word for the disciples. *Mark 9:19 You unbelieving generation," Jesus replied, "how long shall I stay with you? How long shall I put up with you? Bring the boy to me (NLT)."* The sooner we have the difficult conversation, the better. I am an oncologist nurse. I witness firsthand the devastation of cancer on the body. I know it is better to catch cancer early and get rid of it before it spreads and becomes more dangerous. The religious leaders did not like Jesus' answers to their questions. Yet Jesus gave the truth to them even if it appeared to be harsh. If Jesus had to teach unpopular messages then we will too.

The gospel of Jesus Christ is unpopular to some. Some have turned away because the gospel did not fit their lifestyle or theology. When Jesus revealed himself to be the bread of life many found it challenging to receive this teaching. *John 6:60*

Many therefore of his disciples, when they had heard this, said, this is an hard saying; who can hear it? Jesus asked in vs 61 *doth this offend you.* Because of Christ's teachings, many of his disciples walked away and followed him no more. *John 6:66-67 From that time many of his disciples went back, and walked no more with him. Then said Jesus unto the twelve, will ye also go away?* If people will walk away from Jesus they will walk away from you! Therefore stand tall and preach the gospel.

When teaching these unpopular words as leaders we have to teach in love. We can teach in love and be steadfast in our teaching. Speaking an unpopular message may be perceived as being without love. Some individuals will be convicted by the word or even offended to have their weaknesses exposed. We may be perceived as been harsh or mean but our hearts will convey a passion to see the individual grow up in Christ and mature. I was once called mean simply because I told a truth. Many have misunderstood a passage on love covering a multitude of sins. *1 Peter 4:8 And above all things have fervent charity among yourselves: for charity shall cover the multitude of sins.* This scripture does not mean to ignore sin and brush it under the rug. Keeping sin buried and in secret will allow the person to remain in a sinful state. Love desires to empower people to become free. Love covers sin by helping the person acknowledge it. We use the message of the gospel's forgiveness and redemption power to assure them that God will forgive them of all their sins. When we teach with true love, people will receive the truth of God's word. The lost will be won over by the love of Jesus Christ.

If a leader has a passive personality it may be difficult to teach the Bible's complex topics. Passive leaders typically avoid conflict. They have a strong desire for happiness and avoiding dealing with challenging situations. They want to keep people happy even if that means not dealing with difficult topics. Passive leaders will avoid making people unhappy even if they have to be unhappy themselves.

Leaders and pastors with this personality struggle with preaching against sin, making changes, and removing underperforming people. Operating with a passive personality will cause a ministry to be disorganized, out of control and chaotic. If we have passive personalities and desire to succeed as leaders, we have to seek God to make us stronger. If God gives us instructions to teach a word that will anger our followers, focus on the message and not their faces. Tune out their facial expressions and stand on the assignment to please God.

Chapter 10

CALLING FULFILLED

2 Thessalonians 1:11

Wherefore also we pray always for you, that our God would count you worthy of this calling, and fulfill all the good pleasure of his goodness, and the work of faith with power.

Isaiah's calling was fulfilled because of his willingness to serve God despite the difficult assignment. What constitutes a fulfilled calling? Growing a mega church and having millions in the bank is an incredible achievement. It's powerful to be able to dissect the word of God, breaking it down into the Hebrew and Greek languages. Performing miracles, signs and wonders are also incredible acts. While all of these achievements are wonderful, they do not represent having our call fulfilled.

A calling fulfilled is living sold out totally for Jesus Christ. He has to work on us, his servants, before we can lead others. It may be popular to desire to work for Christ and seek personal gain. A true shepherd does not work for hire. If we work for hire, we will eventually run, give up, quit during times of great hardship. Jesus said in *John 10:11-12 I am the good shepherd: the good shepherd giveth his life for the sheep. But he that is a hireling, and not the shepherd, whose own the sheep are not, seeth the wolf coming, and leaveth the sheep, and fleeth: and the wolf catcheth them, and they scattereth.* Jesus gave his life for his sheep. To fulfill our calling, we continue to seek the mission God set before us despite the toughness of the assignment, the harsh conditions, the attacks, obstacles and roadblocks. We ignore the circumstance and finish our course. We work for Christ from a pure heart. When we serve from our heart, we go places we would not necessarily choose to go. We say what we are told even when it's difficult.

Many leaders and pastors choose what we want to preach and teach. We stay neutral so we do not offend anyone and it will keep us from our assignment.

Peter, Paul, and Stephen were attacked because of their boldness to tell the truth. We can expect persecution as well. This calling is a labor intensive mission. It is a physically, mentally and ritually laborious. But if we remain steadfast and complete the call on our life, our labor will not be in vain. *1 Corinthians 15:58 Therefore, my beloved brethren, be ye steadfast, unmovable, always abounding in the work of the Lord, forasmuch as ye know that your labour is not in vain in the Lord.*

God's assignment does not have a retirement package. We continue our commission until we die whether we are pastors, leaders, missionaries, or ministers. We will always be a witness to God's word and goodness. When Jesus completed his ministry on earth he went to the cross. It is finished, he said. What an achievement to start and finish well. When the twelve apostles completed their assignments, they rested from their labor. When Elijah was coming to the end of his assignment, God told him to place his mantle on Elisha to become his successor. When Jacob knew his time on earth was coming to an end, he prepared to pass the blessings to his sons. As we read throughout the Bible, we see as one life was ending, they always prepared the next generation to lead. Paul prepared Timothy to be his successor.

We are to prepare the next generation to replace us. We are not to be afraid to pass the mantle. Pastors can end the growth of a church when a successor is not chosen to carry the torch. When a successor is not trained or appointed while the pastor is still living, the congregation is left to wrestle with naming a new leader after the pastor dies. In the haste to name a new leader, mistakes are often made. I believe God gives the existing pastor the name of his or her successor. To share the successor's name with the current leadership team is important in executing God's plan. There is no shame or fear in promoting the next generation to take our place. We have lived a long blessed life and carried out God's plan. At the set time Abraham stepped aside for Isaac. Isaac stepped aside for Jacob. Jacob stepped aside for the twelve tribes of Israel.

When we fulfill our assignment there will be a sense of satisfaction and accomplishment. Have you ever had a big project in school and when you finally completed the assignment you felt a sense of happiness and joy? When we have carried out God's will for our life we will be peace. It is when we do not finish our course, we begin to feel an uneasy.

We have heard someone say "I know I was supposed to carry that out but I didn't?" Let's not find ourselves singing the couldas, wouldas and shouldas. We are unfulfilled when we are not carrying out our assignments. Many have ruined the call of God on their life choosing the pleasures of this world. They are not fully satisfied. The Bible states in *Proverbs 19:21 You can make many plans but the Lord's purpose will prevail (NLT).* The joy of completion will outshine any of the challenges that we encounter along the way. Our reward is greater than the challenges we face. *Romans 8:18 For I reckon that the sufferings of this present time are not worthy to be compared with the glory which shall be revealed in us.*

Joy comes when we obey the voice of God, fulfill the calling on our life, and utilize the gifts he has put in us. No matter what the adversary throws at us, we will remain on top if we continue with God. *2 Peter 1:10 Wherefore the rather, brethren, give diligence to make your calling and election sure: for if ye do these things, ye shall never fall.* We will not fall and God will increase us by making room for the gifts he put in us. *Proverbs 18:16 .A man's gift maketh room for him, and bringeth him before great men.* Spiritual men are not the only great men. Secular men can be great and unbelievers can be great. God creates change agents come from all walks of life. God can place his servants anywhere to deliver his message. We may stand before a great secular musical artist to witness for Jesus Christ. God will elevate us, bless us and prosper us because we are fulfilling his will. We are not to be selfish with blessing. God blesses us to bless others. We offer the light of Jesus Christ to a dark world. All throughout the word of God we will find those who stayed the course, obeyed God and carried out the assignment set before them. They prospered here on earth; *2 Chronicles 26:5 ...and as long as he sought the Lord, God made him to prosper.* Our blessings are not only for heaven; however. heaven has an even greater reward.

We can expect to prosper here on earth when we are faithful to God's will. Many kings that God appointed over Israel prospered as long as they stayed faithful to God's will. When they disobeyed God by worshipping idol gods and engaging in sinful activities, they began to fall and lose focus on their purpose.

Love plays a vital role in fulfilling God's assignment in our life. We are not able to truly know the love of God until we know him intimately. Relationships will not last if true love is not present. Our calling will not be fulfilled if the love of God is not in our heart. Marriage is a symbol of this love. When married couples establish a close intimate relationship their marriage, it will outlast the hard times. Pastors and leaders carry God's love to hurting sheep. Jesus asked Peter three times "do you love me?" Three times Jesus told Peter to feed his sheep (John 21:15-17). The leading and feeding of God's people is directly connected to the love of Christ. Jesus loved the church so much that he married her! *Revelation 19:7 Let us rejoice and be glad and give glory to him for the marriage of the Lamb (Jesus, Bridegroom) has come and his bride (church) has made herself ready.*

Jesus was also married to the backsliders. *Jeremiah 3:14(a) Turn, O backsliding children saith the Lord: for I am married unto you.* True love will go after the lost sheep or family member. God's leaders carry his heart. *Jeremiah 3:15 And I will give you pastors according to mine heart which shall feed you with knowledge and understanding.*

A fulfilled life is a sacrificial life. A sacrificial life is not a life where Jesus is simply added to our agenda, but he is our agenda. Jesus desires for us to live a joyous and happy life here on earth. When Jesus called for his disciples they dropped their secular careers. Jesus became their career. Men and women are leaving their lucrative positions making six figures to follow the call of Christ. This is a sacrificial. I desire to spend more time with God and study his word. I look forward to the day that I too will be able to sacrifice my entire life to the work of the ministry. When we have sacrificed our life for God, we will find that we cannot participate in activities that others may enjoy.

We have to gain balance in our participation in television entertainment, social media entertainment, sports, and movie attendance. When God has a great calling or mission on our life,, we have to focus our efforts on the spiritual disciplines to nourish our souls. God had a special calling and mission for Samson the Nazirite. He was not able to participate in certain activities. Nazirite means consecrated or separated. Samson was set apart to be different and because of this calling he was not able to drink any wine or strong drink. He could not eat grapes or any fruit from a vine. He could not cut his hair and he could not touch any dead bodies (Numbers 6:1-7). This sanctification kept Samson holy to God as long as he was obedient.

John the Baptist was set aside for God's calling. Before he was born he was dedicated for the preparation of the coming Jesus Christ. John the Baptist lived in the wilderness separated from the common population. His calling required a period of separation. John the Baptist took on the Nazarite lifestyle reframing from many earthly pleasures. To devote myself to the ministry, I spend only a small amount of time watching television. After I come home from work, I find myself reading and studying God's word. I enjoy listening to others teach the gospel. I spend time with God and pray. It comes easily to me. I have an earnest desire to know God so much and I am willing to do whatever is necessary. When I have to enjoy family activities for a few hours, I look forward to heading home to bask in the presence of God. I find myself at work excited for the day to end so I can go in my closet and spend time with the Holy Spirit. I long for time with Christ daily. Worldly influences have lost their luster and significance in my life. My greatest desire is to know God and make him known.

Are you willing to fulfill your calling? Some say it does not take all that. It's been said we need balance in our life. Christ is my balance. The parable of the talents helps us to understand this very fact. Only one of the three servants was given five talents. Are you a five, two or one talent leader? What has God entrusted us with and how much are we willing to sacrifice?

A fulfilled call is accomplished by a leader who endures to the end. We can start a race but can we finish? New Year starts with millions of people who are excited and have great zeal to accomplish great feats. The sad truth is only a few will reach the finish line. Many are called, but few are chosen. King Uzziah did not endure to the end. He began his leadership journey pleasing God. As pride grew in his heart, he did not fulfill his calling. When we arrive in heaven, we will learn how much more God had for us to do in our walk on the earth. We will learn that the plans God had for us were far greater than we had for our own lives. For us to endure to the end we have to endure challenges. Challenges keep the best of us from reaching our January or February goals. It's the obstacles and walls that we have to endure, that keeps us distracted from our goals. Losing weight and eating healthy is a big goal for the New Year. The challenge becomes to exercise and choose the right foods. We have to fight pleasing our flesh when we do not want to go back to the gym. To reach our desired weight, we have to press toward that mark. Pastors and leaders have to press beyond discouragement, loneliness, temptations and a desire to quit. Let us be inspired by *Philippians 3:14 I press toward the mark for the prize of the high calling of God in Christ Jesus.* Some challenges come to strengthen us to continue walking in our calling. Eagles are our role models. When facing storms, they do not turn back. Despite fierce winds and blinding rain, they do not let the storms of this life stop them. Pressing against the raging elements empowers eagles to glide on the wind and enjoy the views that are only seen from mountain tops. If you are facing the winds of a big storm, put on your raincoat, grab your boots, and open up your biggest umbrella. Don't give up. Your umbrella will become your parachute and lift you to the greatest heights. The rainbow awaits us on the other side of the storm. The rainbow is our promise that life will become peaceful again. Putting on the whole armor of God will provide protection for us to fight and fulfill our calling (Ephesians 6:10-18). Our sheep are depending on us to guide them through their storms. We have to overcome our storms to teach others.

God's sheep are precious, tender and fragile; they will wander astray if there is no trained shepherd to guide them. *Jeremiah 50:6 My people hath been lost sheep: their shepherds have caused them to go astray, they have turned them away on the mountains: they have gone from mountain to hill, they have forgotten their resting place.* A good shepherd watches over his flock. Let's fulfill our calling by fulfilling God's plan for us at the set time.

Let's position ourselves for a mighty journey. Prepare to move forward. When Paul heard the call he moved forward and never looked back. Let's not look back like Lot's wife. *Luke 9:62 And Jesus said unto him, no man having put his hand to the plough, and looking back is fit for the kingdom of God.* Take your stand, arise and preach the gospel. *Isaiah 60:1 Arise, shine for thy light is come, and the glory of the Lord is risen upon thee.* We have been chosen for a mighty work. The favor of God is on us. Nehemiah was charged with a great work of rebuilding the walls of Jerusalem, the capital city. He ignored the distracters and focused on his assignment. God will enlarge our house and stretch forth our habitation (Isaiah 54:2). If we live in the presence of the Lord and continue to dwell in the secret place in him, he will send his angels with us as we fulfill our calling and he will make our mission successful. Jesus spoke many times during his teachings how prophecy and the scriptures had to be fulfilled. Jesus' life on earth and the cross was a fulfillment of prophecy. God wants to fulfill his plan in your life too.

The lyrics to the song "A charge to keep I have" by Charles Wesley, sums up the duty of the called servant.

A charge to keep I have

A God to glorify,

A never dying soul to save,

And fit it for the sky.

To serve this present age,

My calling to fulfill:

Oh, may it all my pow'rs engage

To do my Master's will!

In Ephesians 4:1 Paul prayed that our God would count us worthy of this calling. God will count us worthy of the call and fulfill all the good pleasures of his goodness. God is calling all of us to impact this world. Let's answer with a willing heart.

Lord, here am I; send me.

About the Author

Evangelist Karen Harris (also known as Evangelist KK) is a native of Chicago. In 1996, she earned a Bachelor's Degree in Nursing. She continued her education and earned a Master's Degree in Nursing in 2008. Karen has worked in the field of oncology for 20 years administering chemotherapy to cancer patients and specializing in breast cancer. She has participated within the community as a keynote speaker for Breast Cancer Awareness. Currently she is a Clinical Nurse Educator in oncology. She addresses women's ministry groups and spoke on leadership at the Women of Vision and Destiny Ministries, Inc. International Christian Women's Conference in Phoenix, Arizona.

Evangelist Harris was called to God's ministry in December 2000. She is a licensed and ordained minister. She is a teacher, author, and ministry coach educator. Karen is the founder of the H.A.I. (Here Am I) Evangelistic Ministries and H.A.I. School of Ministries.

Having a passion for those called to the five-fold ministry, Karen airs a live social media broadcast entitled Leadership Empowerment. In 2013, Karen graduated from the Living Word Christian Center School of Ministry. She is recognized for her powerful spiritual leadership training and development of ministry leaders for God's kingdom building.

CONTACT INFORMATION

Karen Harris, MSN
karen@haiministries.com

Dedication

This book is dedicated in the memory of my loving brother Michael W. Sims and father Wallace Sims Jr.

Acknowledgements

I would like to thank my family for their tremendous support. I would like to give special thanks to my mother, Beatrice Sims for supporting and encouraging me has I ventured out into an unknown territory. Most of all I thank my Lord and Savior Jesus Christ and the Holy Spirit who guided the content of this book.

Made in the USA
Lexington, KY
19 February 2018